SEARCHING FOR HEALING IN GOD'S BACKYARD

(This is not just another Essential Oil
Bible Study! It's so much more!)

Jessica M. Linhart

BALBOA.
PRESS

A DIVISION OF HAY HOUSE

Balboa Press books may be ordered through booksellers or by contacting:

Balboa Press
A Division of Hay House
1663 Liberty Drive
Bloomington, IN 47403
www.balboapress.com
1 (877) 407-4847

Print information available on the last page.

ISBN: 978-1-9822-0828-8 (sc)
ISBN: 978-1-9822-0829-5 (e)

Balboa Press rev. date: 07/23/2018

CONTENTS

(For Teachers) For each lesson please include the following two statements:

The first one is the most important one:

We don't claim to have all the answers, but we do know the God who does. God owns the reserves of the world and He regulates their employment. He is a God of design, purpose, and order. Our mission and passion is to uncover the debts of the riches found in God's backyard and to suggest these findings to other Christians. Hopefully, to improve the health and welfare of all!

Now for the second one Legal requires:

The following statements have not been approved by the FDA. The products recommended including the essential oils are not intended to diagnose, treat, cure, or prevent disease. Pregnant or lactating mothers and persons with medical problems should consult their doctors.

Oil lamps

Class Script

Teacher's Note:

Remember, as always, even if you are doing this lesson solo or if you are teaching a group of people take prayer request's, pray over the lesson and snacks, provide anointing for the sick, follow the class script, allow students/ group members to experience the essential oils and share their experiences, provide the class objectives, and hopefully schedule your next Bible study. Yes, even if it's a study God has provided for someone else to write you may use it. Writers have different experiences and you just might learn something! You may also obtain a different angle/view on a topic God has already taught you!

If this is our first lesson together I'm honored that God connected us. If we have studied together let's rejoin the garden and stay close to God. I've diligently prayed for you and I to stay close with Christ. He is our only hope. Let's begin our examination in **Matthew chapter 25** and read it in its entirety!

Can you describe this section of scripture in five sentences or less? -

_____

_____

_____

What type of oil?

_____

_____

_____

In this particular scripture many believe that it is not an actual oil. However, according to the history of God's people, an oil that burns well is a ...

_____

_____

_____

In the time of Jesus, people created their own oils from the vegetables in their garden.

Genesis 1:29 ESV

And God said, "Behold, I have given you every plant yielding seed that is on the face of all the earth, and every tree with seed in its fruit. You shall have them for food.

Genesis 9:3 ESV

Every moving thing that lives shall be food for you. And as I gave you the green plants, I give you everything. God's people lived in time era that God lead them to create manmade goods.

The residence of this culture never heard of an electric lamp. They relied on God! God provided their gardens! These people lived hard simple lives compared to us today! We simply go to our kitchens and find some kind of oil. Canola and vegetable are probably the first ones we would grab. This is precisely what we need to understand, God's people had simple means, but vegetables were fairly easy to obtain; even though, grocery stores were not in existence. Perhaps, night vision was one of the first needs of God's people. It's interesting how vegetable oil was created and allowed them the ability to study God's Word at night time.

The inside of the home was about as dim as a 40 watt light bulb. Several homes would have an assortment of oil lamps, because olive oil was in abundance and therefore not expensive. On the other hand, the King James Version of the Bible translates the word for lamp as "candlesticks." Interminably, we must ask the Holy Spirit to interpret scripture for us.

Then, occasionally we have to seek other Historical references to obtain a clear implication. The Bible divulges that we are to study to prove yourself worthy. (**2 Timothy 2:5**) In final regurads, the ancient world they did not use candles. Even the seven branches on the menorah, within the Tabernacle, were actually lamps that held olive oil and wicks. The Holy anointment oil combination was also used in lamps and not candlesticks.

Ancient lamps were oval shaped and flat on top. One end of the wick would even float in the olive oil. Various lamps had a lid over the bowl. The citizens of the lower class made their lamps from clay, but the more expensive lamps were made of bronze and gold. The costly lamps were used in temples and given to emperors. They were beautiful and would contain very elaborate decorations. The crafters of lamps would put images of God for the Hebrews and Roman lamps would have images of their gods.

Lighting a lamp was not as easy as flipping a switch. It was customary to rub two sticks together, or they would strike stones together to trigger a light. The oil of an olive was obtainable in abundance supply; therefore, lamps were also used as air freshers. Intermixing certain oils would provide a sweet aroma; while, combining other oils with olive oil would help heal a cold. For example, the mixture of oils depended on the type of illness they were trying to evade below are a few examples:

Basil essential oil is also used by a lot of people for their digestive issues. Holistic doctors recommend that this essential oil be used for the treatment of indigestion, constipation, stomach cramps and gas the stomach.

Rosemary essential oil is used to treat poison ivy. It is directly applied to the skin with no dilution. I recommend this oil for pregnant mother's. I have even included the oil in baby shower gifts! Rosemary, again not diluted, applied to the belly has been used as an effective stretch mark prevention remedy.

Thyme essential oil is used to help people relieve symptoms of gout, arthritis, wounds, bites, and sores.

Cilantro essential oil can be used to cleans the body if taken as a daily vitamin, several families use this essential oil in dips and salads. For a refreshing herbal aroma mix cilantro and citrus in your lamp!

Oregano essential oil mixed in a lamp can provide soothing allergy relief, to boost your immune system naturally, and it may help keep a cold away.

Spiritually how does Jesus help you see in the dark?

_____

_____

_____

When God grabs you by the right hand and leads you to the promise land; who will be the light of that heavily city?

_____

_____

_____

That's right just like olive oil we need Jesus to see the true world as God see it! Allow God to shine through you! A way to give yourself a checkup: is to ask yourself if you've been asked for prayer, asked if you're a Christian, or if you have been persecuted for proclaiming Jesus. If you can't answer yes to these questions, you have failed the authors test. This does not mean you failed God's test. He came so that we could have ever lasting life. The devil came to seek, steel, and destroy. Please visit God in prayer. Then, please visit a local church, or ask a group member about Christ today! The signs are here dear friend. Christ is ready to return in the Eastern sky! I pray each one of us will be ready!

How can we obtain heaven? This scripture gives us words that can be formulated into a mental picture. In the boxes above draw five braids maids for a wedding. Allow one side to be dressed almost ready; while the other side is missing a few things. Now, under the words, write the spiritual meaning for prepared and unprepared.

Most of society falls into one of the groups of virgins in **Matthew 25.**

Prepared   Unprepared

_____

_____

_____

According to the text: What does it mean to be prepared?

_____

_____

_____

The most important attribute of our image for God is not our appearance, but rather, has the blood of Jesus Christ has been applied. The first group of virgins had oil in their lamps. They even had more oil than what they needed. The second group of foolish braids maids did not have enough oil too last. The spiritual oil is a representation of us believing Jesus was born from a virgin birth, he was crucified on the cross, and he rose again. When we accept these facts about Jesus the Holy spirit rushes into our soul. We are giving the ability to sustain while He is delayed in heaven. So, we have enough oil in our lamps. Our charge is to be the light of the world.

In **verse 7** what did the foolish braids maid complete?

_____

_____

_____

When the unprepared heard the voice of the groom they all jumped up! I remember, when my girls had a slumber party! I awoke them! There was not a bunch of screaming or running! It was more like yawning, stretching, and fuzzing over the bathroom sick. How do think the braid maids would answer a call from Jesus!

_____

_____

_____

In the text, the braids maid trimmed their wicks. Is that what we are doing? Are you allowing Christ to trim your wick?

_____

_____

_____

Of course, the ones who were unprepared asked the prepared to borrow some of their oil. The oil was not theirs to lend. The oil has forever belonged to Christ. Jesus is the oil. I can't give you the relationship I have with Christ and you cannot give me your relationship with Christ. We must save ourselves. We cannot go to heaven because Mom and Dad went to heaven or because our spouse went to heaven. As much as we desire to give our oil, when God closes the door to our enteral home, that's it. There will be no time to go and search for Jesus. Jesus is coming! God the father will become God the Judge.

Examine the following verses! This will prove to you that God wears those two different hats!

The following verse are in
Matthew: 7:1-2, 7:21-23, and 25:31-46.

Matthew: 7:1-2

_____

_____

_____

Matthew: 7:21-23

_____

_____

_____

Matthew: 25:31-46

_____

_____

_____

Next examine **Luke 15:11-32**

_____

_____

_____

Luke 19:11-27

_____

_____

_____

The authors final thoughts:

If you are in Christ, ease your groaning, in knowing that Satan can't touch you! Jesus cut the head off Satan, like he trims our wicks, and like David cut off Goliaths head. (**1 Samuel 17:4**) Jesus can cut off the head of all your problems. (**1 Peter 5:7**) All we have to do is go to an altar of prayer and asked to be delivered. (**Psalm 34:4**) We must keep moving toward the mark! (**Philippians 3:14**) Yesterday, is gone and God brings all anew tomorrow. (**Psalm 103:5**) If you returned to your sin the bible says God describes your situation as a dog returning to his vomit. You will have seven more demons then you had before. (**2 Peter 2:22**) When we mess up; just fess up! Finally, we could set on the side-lines of life, like a lamp with no oil, or we can fill up! Fill-up with the holy spirit! Why stay in your sin sick life? Get your light to shine. Join the winning team!

1 Samuel 17:4

_____

_____

_____

1 Peter 5:7

_____

_____

_____

Psalm 34:4

_____

_____

_____

Philippians 3:14

_____

_____

_____

Psalm 130:5

_____

_____

_____

2 Peter 2:22

_____

_____

_____

The Good Samaritan

Class Script

Read **Luke 10:34-42** in the King James Version. Then, read **Luke in 10:34** in The Living Bible. King James Version records the Biblical occurrence in detail. The Living Bible records less details, but this version is great to use if you just need to be reminded of the story.

Why was this story included in the scripture?

_____

_____

_____

What is the meaning of a Good Samaritan?

_____

_____

_____

Several people totally miss Jesus's point of the parable. Sure, most of the world considers this parable as someone who does good for someone else and all of society knows this definition, but God's people understand the hidden meaning. Jesus told these parables to confound the four political parties of his time and because he knew this story would confound the foolish until He returns. This parable like many of the other parables was meant to teach salvation. How many facts point to salvation from this scripture? (Hints: We are fifthly rags, in need of a savior, putting on the new man, loving others as we love ourselves, and even going the extra mile.)

_____

_____

_____

_____

_____

_____

Allow me to state the obvious: A Good Samaritan is someone who helps a stranger. However, A Good Samaritan is also considered as a member of a people inhabiting the land named Samaria in biblical times. In addition, in our modern community, Samara is the region of Nablus. A Samaritan claims to be a descent from them, but that they still adheres to a form of Judaism accepting only its own ancient version of the Pentateuch as Scripture.

Side Note: The Pentateuch is Arabic for the first books of the Bible. It is also known as the Torah for the Jews.

It's interesting to know that we have Good Samaritan Laws for our society today. What does the law ensure someone who helps a stranger?

_____

_____

_____

According to https://en.wikipedia.org/wiki/Good_Samaritan_law, "Good Samaritan laws offer legal protection to people who give reasonable assistance to those who are, or who they believe to be, injured, ill, in peril, or otherwise incapacitated. The protection is intended to reduce bystanders' hesitation to assist, for fear of being sued or prosecuted for unintentional injury or wrongful death."

If you read **Luke 10:29** you can quickly see why the story is revealed in the Bible. Jesus was teaching and a man that asked Jesus who is my neighbors and should I love them? Jesus then told the men the story of the Good Samaritan as an example. The story is included in the Bible for our learning as well. Jesus wants us to realize how He wants us to love our neighbors. Jesus also wants us to realize who He identifies as are neighbors.

Is there a neighbor that you do not love? Ask God to reveal them to you and then ask the Holy Spirit to help you love them? One the space below record one nice act you could do for them that shows love.

_____

_____

_____

Who was the victim?

_____

_____

Why did the Jewish priest and the temple helper pass by him?

_____

_____

Did Jesus agree with this behavior? Why or why not?

_____

_____

Where was, the injured man laying? Was he hidden?

_____

_____

Describe the acts of kindness given to the injured?

_____

_____

_____

How was the injured anointed?

_____

_____

_____

Why did the Jews and Sanitarians hate each other?

_____

_____

_____

The example Jesus gave took place on a road between Jerusalem and Jericho. Over the last several years I've heard about this dangerous road. In one of my past books we even discovered this route as being a trading route. Many people were hurt and even killed over the goods they carried along this road. The scripture did not state why the rubbers targeted this man. The scriptures only state that they tore his clothes, took his belongings, and left him to die. Jesus also did not state if the injured was an enemy, a foreigner, a Jew, or a Samaritan. I guess Jesus did not care about the man's ethic background. And why just He? God made everything, but man put His creation into sections. In addition, God shows no favoritism or partiality, and the Bible teaches us that we should not either. "Yes indeed, it is good when you truly obey our Lord's royal command found in the Scriptures: 'Love your neighbor as yourself.' But if you pay special attention to the rich, you are committing sin, for you are guilty of breaking that law" (**James 2:1-4, 8-9**). Furthermore, many of Peter's fellow Jews thought that God loved them more than the gentiles, but Peter came to understand that God did not show favoritism. God wants people of all nations to repent and be saved (**2 Peter 3:9; 1 Timothy 2:4**).

The apostle Paul explained that the time order of God's plan was not a sign of injustice or favoritism. "There will be trouble and calamity for everyone who keeps on sinning—for the Jew first and also for the Gentile. But there will be glory and honor and peace from God for all who do good—for the Jew first and also for the Gentile. For God does not show favoritism" (**Romans 2:9-11**, New Living Translation).

During this time period Samaritans were hated by the Jews and the Jews hated the Samaritans. There were many reasons why the two groups hated each other. A couple of reasons the two groups fought was over land and the placing of their temples. The Samaritans fought against the rebuilding the Jewish temple in Jerusalem. The Samaritans also had discontentment for the Jews, because the Jews tore down their temple at Mount Gerizim. Mount Gerizim was located in Nablus. Mount Gerizim is the oldest mountain range in the world. The Samaritans still worship God there today.

Jesus was speaking to the Jew in this scripture. He specifically placed the Samaritan in the story! Was there a reason for that?

_____

_____

_____

Probably, the Jews never spoke about how good the Samaritans were. The Jews hated them. They did not spread the good about a Smartian because they did not look for any good thing in them. This story got them scratching their head. They probably thought could Jesus tell us someone else to love? Anyone besides that group of people?

They did not want to discuss that a Samaritan performed this heroic deed. The Samaritan traveled the same road and saw the man lying beside the road. I wondered if he questioned whether to help the injured man. I wonder if he weighted -out the consequences of his actions. In the chart below list a few pros and cons about helping the injured man. This time, there are no right or wrong answers. This activity, will teach you how to think outside the box.

Pros: Cons:

Most people believe the Samaritan simply saw a need and tried to fulfill the need. In biblical days, essential oils were always toted along. Similarly, to us carrying along a first aid kit. The road from Jerusalem to Jericho was very dangerous; therefore, it makes perfect sense that the Good Samaritan was carrying his first aid kit.

What do you think was in the Good Samaritans first aid kit?

Without a doubt, you should include: Lavender, Tea Tree, Peppermint, Roman Chamomile, Eucalyptus, Rosemary, Thyme, Lemon, and Clove bud.

Helichrysum: Bruising Swelling Injury: bruising, sprains It will reduce the discoloration and help heal the bruise very quickly. Because it has analgesic properties bumps and bruises won't be as painful.	Lavender: bites, bruises, sleep, allergies, inflammation, sunburns, and lice **Simple First Aid Wash** Simply put several drops of Lavender essential oil in a small basin of tepid water.	Peppermint: Nausea, digestive, Peppermint also helps with headaches, sinus congestion and even for painful joints! Add five drops to calamine lotion to relieve and heal Poison.	Oregano: Kills warts, skin tags, athlete's foot Inhale directly: opens up the airways. Sore throat: Add a few drops of oregano oil to a glass of warm water and gargle with the blend.
Tea Tree Oil Good for all types of infections. Great for all kinds of skin wounds and irritations from sunburn, to acne, and athlete's feet.	**Eucalyptus** Relieves congestion from coughs and colds. Helps stimulate the feelings to calm down.	**Lemon** will freshen and clean most all surfaces. Can be very effective on insect bites. Some folks have found headache relief from using Lemon oil too. Add one drop to your water for a fresh new drink. Great for avoiding the high cost of a restaurant beverage.	**Clove Bud** It is great for toothaches and other pains, such as painful joints and muscles. Add to lattes for an extra kick.

How did the Good Samaritan treat the injured? He anointed the man by either pouring the oil drops right out of the flask or by pouring the ointment onto rags and rubbing his wounds. As recorded in Luke, the Good Samaritan lifts him unto his donkey and takes him to the nearest Inn. As if this was enough! He stays the night with the injured man and continues to treat his lesions.

How do you think the Good Samaritan treats the wounds of the injured man?

_____

_____

_____

The Good Samaritan would have treated the injuries with cold and warm compresses. He would have fed the injured man, prayed, and burned air purifying essential oils to cleanse the room. His treatment would have required supervision all night. Let's look at the following treatment plan: According to the 7th edition of the Modern Essentials usage guide, on a wound place one to three drops of helichrysum on fresh wound. Add one drop of clove to help reduce pain. Once bleeding has stopped, apply a drop of lavender (to help start healing), a drop of melaleuca (to help fight infection), and drop of lemongrass (for possible ligament damage.) Bandage the wound by soaking each strip of fabric into warm water infused with the oils. When changing the bandage apply one drop of basil, sandalwood, and frankincense to help promote further healing. Finally, adding one drop of a cleansing blend or protective blend would help prevent infection.

Below, are the steps to a great Essential Oil treatment plan.

1. Clean yourself and then clean the injured. (Use a simple First aide wash-mentioned above.)
2. Stop any bleeding by creating a compress of cypress (bleeding), lavender (cleaning and stop bleeding), and melaleuca (Tea-Tree Oil-infection)
3. Bandage the wound by soaking each strip of fabric into warm water infused with the oils of Chamomile, Eucalyptus (calming and airways), and myrrh (decrease infections).
4. Repeat as needed, but the second bandages should be with sandalwood (calming, swelling, and bruising), oregano (to open airways), and frankincense (to create new skin).

Then, the Good Samaritan saved the life of this injured man. Then, the Good Samaritan goes the extra mile and pays for his room until he's well.

After reading this lesson what is Jesus expecting us to be like?

_____

_____

_____

To answer the question, who is our neighbor? This author understands, this to mean, our neighbor is anyone who we encounter. For example, our neighbor is anyone we see during the day. Jesus requires us to treat anyone we see with compassion and kindness. For example, while my family was walking in our neighborhood we witnessed a woman falling in her driveway. We stopped, but a man beat us to the punch. All we did was stop quietly and pray. After, completing this lesson, I realized I needed to go the extra mile and follow-up with her. Friends, it's hard to have Christ's mind when we are in our flesh, but let's not let this be our excuse for not doing the right thing. This week ask God to help you love your neighbor as yourself.

Today, we see several charities who are naming themselves as Good Samaritans. A Few to mention, but not a conclusive list includes: Samaritan's Purse, Sisters of the Good Samaritan, The Good Smartian Hospital, The

Samaritan Befrienders and more. Below is a list so that you can further investigate the organizations.

Samaritan's Purse,

_____

_____

_____

Sisters of the Good Samaritan,

_____

_____

_____

The Good Smartian Hospital,

_____

_____

_____

The Samaritan Befrienders,

_____

_____

_____

You can find other parables in God's word that responds to who is my neighbor and who should I love? If you would like to investigate further start with these scriptures: **Leviticus 19:18** and **Matthew 5:43-48.**

_____

_____

_____

Jessica's Family Blend

First Aide Blend Room Spritzier	Focus	Muscle Tension	Immune Support Hand Sanitizer	Sleepy Time
Lavender Melaleuca Fractionated Coconut oil www. FindingHealingIn GodsBackyard. Com	Orange Grapefruit Fractionated Coconut Oil www. FindingHealingIn GodsBackyard. Com "Energize the mind for mental clarity, focus & memory" Your body absorbs what you put on it. Use only high quality, therapeutic grade oils.	Roman Chamomile Peppermint, Ylang Ylang, "Message into skin after an intense workout." "Provides a cooling and soothing sensation to targeted areas." www. FindingHealingIn Godsbackyard.com	Orange Clove Bud Eucalyptus "Supports immune system to product against environmental threats." www. FindingHealingIn Godsbackyard.com	Lavender Roman Chamomile Fractionated Coconut oil "Dab on bad of neck, earlobes, under nose, bottoms of feet" www. FindingHealingIn Godsbackyard.com
Tummy Trouble	**Stress Less**	**Happy-Perfume**	**Hand Soap**	**Sting Relief**
Peppermint Ginger Lemon Grass "Eases digestive discomfort, bloating, cramps, etc." Apply to tummy or bottoms of the feet. www. FindingHealingIn GodsBackyard. Com	Geranium Chamomile Basil Rose "Promotes a sense of calmness, peace, feeling, grounded & soothing." www. FindingHealingIn GodsBackyard. Com	Peppermint Mint Lavender clary sage tangerine "Promotes happy mood with energizing uplifting properties." "Dab on bad of neck, earlobes, under nose, bottoms of feet" www. FindingHealingIn Godsbackyard.com	Orange Clove Eucalyptus "For those times when there ain't no soap." Boosts Immune Can apply all over body including your hair. www. FindingHealingIn Godsbackyard.com	Lemon Lavender Thyme Eucalyptus "Apply to sting with an ice-cold compress." www. FindingHealingIn Godsbackyard.com

Plus: My All-Natural Bug Spray, clean gulls, and tape.

CLASS 3

THE TOMB OF JESUS

CLASS SCRIPT

The first one is the most important one:

We don't claim to have all the answers, but we do know the God who does. God owns the reserves of the world and He regulates their employment. He is a God of design, purpose, and order. Our mission and passion is to uncover the debts of the riches found in God's backyard and to suggest these findings to other Christians. Hopefully, to improve the health and welfare of all!

Now for the second one Legal requires:

The following statements in this book and spoken in class have not been approved by the FDA. The products recommended including the essential oils are not intended to diagnose, treat, cure, or prevent disease. Pregnant or lactating mothers and persons with medical problems should consult their doctors.

Teachers Note:

Be sure to take prayer request, if having food/drink please say grace, and pray for God to teach. If you allow the Holy Spirit to teach – you don't have too.

Author's Picks:

— Be sure to present <u>eucalyptus, frankincense, and myrrh</u> essential oil during class.

— If you have a diffuser be sure to pour in a couple drops of eucalyptus essential oil.

— Today's scriptures come from the **John 19:38-42 ESV** and it is written here for your convenience.

Jesus Is Buried

[38] After these things Joseph of Arimathea, who was a disciple of Jesus, but secretly for fear of the Jews, asked Pilate that he might take away the body of Jesus, and Pilate gave him permission. So, he came and took away his body. [39] **Nicodemus also, who earlier had come to Jesus by night, came bringing a mixture of myrrh and aloes, about seventy-five pounds in weight.** [40] So they took the body of Jesus and bound it in linen cloths with the spices, as is the burial custom of the Jews. [41] Now in the place where he was crucified there was a garden, and in the garden a new tomb in which no one had yet been laid. [42] So because of the Jewish day of Preparation, since the tomb was close at hand, they laid Jesus there.

The Gospel of John records that Joseph, a member of the Sanhedrin, had to boost his morel, before going to ask for Jesus's body. One reason Joseph could have been afraid is possibly that he felt guilty for not standing up for Jesus. The second reason Joseph had to muster-up some courage before approaching Pilate was because, Pilate had the power to put him on the cross. Can you think of any more reasons Joseph would have his heart full of fear?

_____

_____

_____

Next let's consider another scripture. Please inspect **Luke 24:1**.

What did **Luke 24:1** state?

_____

_____

_____

Luke's account utilized special sources to convey what happened on the day of our Saviors resurrection. Doctor Luke took a considerable portion of his portion from Joanna and the other followers present at this account. Historians believe that the holy women were divided into two companies. These two companies arrived separately at the sepulcher. St. Luke's announcement here denotes that the party (of women) arrived secondly at the tomb. This seems the first group included the two Maries and the other group included Joanna and the others.(**Luke 24:10**) The reason for this thought is based on the fact that they could not purchase their spices on Sabbath (**Luke 24:1**). Therefore, the two groups of ladies had to be divided in order to take part in the same work. Jesus died on a Friday; therefore, the women knew Saturday was church and no stores would be open for part of the weekend.

Side Note: Jewish Burial Practices:

Jews lived in the Mesopotamian areas. Their utmost fear was being buried uncovered. The Jewish textbooks that I read denoted the following: "May the earth not receive your corpses." In addition, in our text (the Bible) states that the Israelites attached their fear to a statement that they feared being left unburied. Thus, one of the curses to breach the covenant is: "Thy carcasses shall be food unto all fowls of the air, and unto the beasts of the earth" (**Deut. 28:26**). Again, and again the prophets use this threat, especially Jeremiah. He says, in judgment on King Jehoiakim, "He shall be buried with the burial of an ass, drawn and cast forth beyond the gates of Jerusalem" Thus, we know that only the criminals were thrown away like animals. Hence, it intrigues me that Pilate gave the body of Jesus to Joseph. Perhaps, he felt guilty, knew he was not guilty, or perhaps it was Godly persuasion. On the other hand, this is why Adolf Hitler left the bodies of the Jews uncover or burned. He treated them as less than animals and this action was truly a slap in the face.

Jews only perform cremations a few times. The people wanted to be in the toms of their fathers. The religious sector of the Jews did not condemn the practice. I could not locate archaeological evidence that this was their practice. Of course, I consulted our text and the following references to "burnings" were imputed to me. Check out the funeral for certain kings. (**Jer. 34:5; II Chron. 16:14; 21:19**) These scriptures report that there was burning of incense and some of the king's possessions, but not his body.

Another burial practice that was important to the Jews was being in their native land and placed with one's ancestors. What did Jacob request? (**Genesis 49:29**)

This statement was burned into the heart of the ancient Israelite.
What were David's wishes for burial?

I believe in 1 Kings 2:10 David makes the following claim: "that I may die in mine own city, [and be buried] by the grave of my father and of my mother"

The desires of a religious Jewish family were to be buried in the family's graveyard. The graveyard was located out of town. Bodies would be laid on rock shelves provided on three sides of the chamber, and as generations of the same family passed their skeletons and grave goods were heaped up along the sides. We find evidence of this both with Jesus's barrowed tomb, but also in **Genesis 25:8.**

---

2 Kings 23:6 and Jer. 26:23 ensures that even the commoner like the hungry were showed respect by being given a spot. The phrase, "to sleep with one's fathers" and "to be gathered to one's kin" is expressed in **Gen. 25:8.**

Jesus Christ fit into the category of being poor and he did not have a family plot in the region where he was crucified. As an act of honor and respect Jesus was placed in a new tomb. Joseph of Arimathea's provided a tomb for Jesus' body. The ladies washed and wrapped the body of Jesus and placed inside the tomb. The entrances to the tombs was closed to protect His body from wild animals.

The following situations are described in scripture. I have written the occurrence and your job is to locate the chapter and verse.

1. _____ Abraham and Sarah were buried in a cave called Machpelah. Abraham purchased this cave from a Hittite so that he and his family could have a burial place.
2. _____ Deborah, Rebekah's nurse, was buried under a tree.
3. _____ Jacob was placed in the tomb of his father Abraham. Issac, Rebekah and Leah were also buried here.
4. _____ The bones of Joseph were taken from Egypt during the Israelites exodus and buried in a field.

Why was spices and essential used for the burial Jesus?

The aromatic perfumes and balms used in burials had a twofold purpose. First, the most obvious reason perfumes and aromatic balms were use was to mask the predictable odor of the decaying. The other intention was associated with the chemical properties in the essential oils. The essential oils would have slowed the process of decaying and would have protected the body from insect scavengers.

How was spices and essential used for the burial of Jesus?

Not only was Jesus' body prepared according to Jewish burial customs, but they received this process from in Egyptians way before the rule of the Romans. The diseased body was typically wrapped in shrouds which were either sprinkled or pasted with aromatic resins and perfumes. The shrouds were most often strips of fabric, but in some instances whole strips of linen (a sheet) were used to wrap the deceased. Theses shreds were also the same as the rags used for birthing. Archaeological evidence reveals that plant essences from pine and frankincense were used in the preparing the body.

Species belonging to the 23 species of pine, frankincense, and terebinth. (Terebinth is a small southern European tree of the cashew family that was formerly a source of turpentine.) were important in burial rituals, because either as a symbol of mourning, and as means of preparation for burial. In addition, the aromatic perfumes and resins used in burials had a dual purpose. First, the more obvious reason to use perfumes and aromatic resins is to mask the inevitable smell of decay. Secondly, it is related to the chemical properties of the oils, which slow the process of decay and protect the body from insect rummaging.

According to well preserved bodies of the Egyptians who were embalmed; we discovered that their organs removed and stuffed with natron. A natron is a simple form of salt made up of sodium bicarbonate and sodium carbonate. Then, the linen cloths and bandages were soaked in essential oils. (a powdered form at the time of Joseph's embalming) After, 40 days the body shrink, because of drying. The natron was removed and replaced with fresh packages of sawdust, plant extracts: such as, onions, myrrh, frankincense, cassia, cinnamon, and other aromatic oils. Next, to seal the body beeswax and hot oils were applied to the body. In addition, balms included wood oils, spices, perfumes and aromatic oils. We find an instance of this type of burial in Genesis 50:2 and 50: 26. Finally, the essential oils, are antibacterial, antiseptic, and antifungal. These properties would have preserved the remains longer than the natural process.

What process did the Egyptians teach Moses?
What are the steps in the process?

1. Washing of the body is done by the family.
2. The family takes his body to Nickideous for purification.
3. Remove internal organs and fill it with natron.
4. They, gather strips of linen or whole sheets of linen.
5. Archaeological evidence reveals that plant essences from pine and frankincense were used in the preparing the body.
6. After 40 days the natron was extracted and filled with oils of wood and sawdust.
7. The saturated the rags with essential oils of myrrh, Frankincense, cassia, and other wood oils.

The family was then given back the body to adorn with jewels and to be placed in the family's tomb.

Who brought the spices?

_____

_____

_____

Mary Magdalene, Joanna, Mary the mother of James, and other women came to Jesus's entombment prepared to perform their custom of burial. **John 19:40** states that Jesus was buried in accordance to all Jewish laws. First, Jesus would have been given a bath by the women. Then, the women would have torn long pieces of fabric and dipped them in aloe and myrrh. The women would have said their Jewish prayer. Much similar to us reciting our Psalm 23 scripture. Finally, they would have put his body on a rock shelf or ledge in a cave.

Based on the information above what were the
steps in the Jewish custom for burial?

1.   5.

2.   6.

3.   7.

4.   8.

We have all been to the graveyard! When we go there we are looking for the dead not the living. The women had just witness the cruelty Jesus had taken. They all saw Him carry his cross, the placement of the crown of thorns, the nails, the piercing of His side, the removal of his body, and then a bare cross for three days. They had no idea that the bare cross meant we would be free from sin. It took the shedding of blood, from the Lamb of God, to reconcile mankind. Today, in many Jewish graveyards they have a hired grave attendant that lives on the ground. Their job is to make sure all Jewish laws are met.

Opps! I got a little ahead! Let's go back and review how the priests and Joseph were able to get the body of Jesus. Read **Matthew 27:62-66!**

Matthew 27:62-66 62The next day, the one after Preparation Day, the chief priests and the Pharisees went to Pilate. 63 "Sir," they said, "we remember that while he was still alive that deceiver said, 'After three days I will rise again.' 64So give the order for the tomb to be made secure until the third day. Otherwise, his disciples may come and steal the body and tell the people that he has been raised from the dead. This last deception will be worse than the first." 65 "Take a guard," Pilate answered. "Go, make the tomb as secure as you know how." 66So they went and made the tomb secure by putting a seal on the stone and posting the guard.

Who sealed the tomb of Jesus?

_____

_____

_____

Nicodemus was a very rich man. He was an undertaker in the village. He was the one who provided the aloes and myrrh for the deaths in his community. Therefore, Nicodemus had all the burial oils stored in a warehouse. Nicodemus loved Jesus, but he was secret about it, because he was afraid of what man would do to him. He may even have feared he would lose his business and his family. But on this day, Nicodemus showed how much he loved Jesus. Nicodemus provided seventy-five pounds of burial ointment and spices to ensure Jesus was treated as royalty. That is like 75, 1-gallon, jugs of milk. Since, he was such a rich man I believe he also had servants. Nicodemus had to have help carrying seventy-five pounds of aloe and myrrh.

God with His perfect plan used all the Jewish laws to keep Satan from creating doubt around the resurrection. First, God made sure there were two men of power burying His son. Then, the body was seen prepared as all other burials, but in a new tomb so there would be no other bodies to confuse man. Thirdly, the tomb was guarded to ensure no one stole Jesus's body.

Why was Jesus to be buried alone?

_____

_____

_____

Your right! So, there could be no mistake in the identification of Jesus. Read **2 Kings 11:23** and **Genesis 25:8** for further evidence.

What other precise plans were delivered to ensure there would be no doubt Jesus was crucified, buried, and arose?

_____

_____

_____

Here are three other areas to consider:

1. The same witnesses returned the day of the resurrection.
2. Who witnessed Jesus after his resurrection?

_____

_____

    -How many?

_____

3. How about his folded napkin?

_____

_____

_____

The Jews were all about their customs and signs. The Jews after they were excused from eating a meal they would fold their napkins. The folding of their napkin sent a signal to their slaves and servants. The folded napkin was a signal that told them to leave their plate and they would return to finish.

Who found Jesus's folded napkins and clothes?

_____

_____

_____

Now, when the women came to the empty tomb. They must have imagined the worst, but God provided the witnesses. Women were viewed as foolish. So, it was no surprise that when they came to tell Peter he did not believe them. Then, Peter runs to the tomb to see for himself. In the above passage, we find Peter kneeling to find the folded napkin.

Now that we have determined Jesus died, buried, and arose you have received the gospel. The Bible says in order to be saved you must have heard the gospel and believe it all. Then, you have to repent and turn from your sin. Finally, you must ask Him to come in your heart and set up camp. If you were saved today, please notify the author of your confession that Christ is Lord. She just wants to rejoice with you and pray for you. Be sure to get in a church that will teach you about the Lord and encourage you to be a good disciple.

Finally, let's examine myrrh and aloes. Jesus was followed by myrrh throughout his life. Once at his birth, once when he was hanging on the cross, and there is no doubt He witnessed the use of myrrh during His childhood. Below match the verse to the scripture.

Matthew 2:11   And they offered him wine mixed with myrrh, but he did not take it.

John 19:39   Nicodemus also, who earlier had come to Jesus by night, came bringing a mixture of myrrh and aloes, about seventy-five pounds in weight.

Mark 15:23   opening their treasures, they offered him gifts, gold and frankincense and myrrh.

Aloes have great aromas. I have read that there are over 500 plants of Aloe Vera. Today, we even have an Aloe Vera tree in India. The tree can grow as tall as one hundred feet. When the tree is harvested its cut into wood The wood contains secretions of Aloe Vera essential oil. The essential oil of aloe smells fabulous and keeps the wood from rotting. If I lived in India and had access to this wood I would use the wood to line the walls in my cabinet. I can also see the benefit in the bathroom, because of all the moisture.

What is aloe essential oil?

_____

_____

_____

Today, we make an Aloe Vera gel. I'm sure everyone reading this book has used this gel for a sunburn. If not, the Aloe Vera gel rapidly sooths the skin. The gel helps the skin from peeling. Aloe puts moisture in the skin; which, also might reduce scars and wrinkles. I have suffered from acne all my life and in high school I grew my first aloe plant. I popped open each leaf and rubbed the oil directly on my acne. I can't say it removed my acne, but it did reduce the soreness. However, I am extremely allergic to poison ivy and I can vouch that fresh aloe from the plant healed my rash overnight. Some people, use Aloe Vera to reduce the effects of their psoriasis, eczema, and rashes. Finally, aloe has been in hair care products for many years. People have reported aloe makes their hair strong, made their hair grow, and even has stopped dry itchy scalp.

What have you used aloe Vera plants to treat your skin?

_____

_____

_____

THE SHIELD

CLASS SCRIPT

Teachers Note:

Be sure to take prayer requests, if having food/drink please say grace, and pray for God to teach. If you allow the Holy Spirit to teach – you don't have too. Be sure to assign the scriptures before class commences and allow the students to read it during class. Also, make sure you allow students to respond to the questions before you provide the answer the questions.

_____

_____

_____

God's people made the first shield from animals skins. Then man learned how to chisel stone and concrete to create a shield. About 2000 years ago Roman soldiers (Paul which was Saul) carried shields made of iron and wood. Which one would you want to carry?

_____

We should be thankful that we don't have to carry such a magnitude. My friends, I've always alleged that, "A Christian's Faith fights all battles." The shield of faith is more than a weapon. It's with your faith that kingdoms are defeated, mountains are moved, and biblical promises are fulfilled. Nevertheless, if your shield is anointed, your transformed, and ready for battle.

Today's class focuses on the following scripture:

2,000 years ago the people knew and understood the purpose of the attire the soldiers wore. Just like today we understand the need to provide our military with necessary supplies. So then, why are we surprised that as "God's Soldiers" we have to also be equipped.

Turn to **Ephesians 6:16:** Above all, taking the shield of faith, wherewith ye shall be able to quench all the fiery darts of the wicked.

Paul was born off the south coast of Turkey which was the town of Tarsus. Saul was born in 5 A.D. From the age of six he learned the Torah. He was taught their customs and laws. He lived with the Greeks which were pagans. When Saul was about 14 his family sent him to Jerusalem to further his studies. Jerusalem was the capital and was King Solomon built the tabernacle and the arc of the covenant was there. The laws of the Jews were set in stone and Jesus defied the laws. Therefore, Saul made it is personal mission to wipe the name of Jesus off the face of the Earth. Saul then began killing all who followed Christ. Saul even killed Steven. He marched him out of the temple and gave the word for him to be stoned to death. Steven prayed that Saul would come to know Christ. (**Acts 6:8-8:1**) Paul traveled all of Galilee and the surrounding cities hunting the Followers of Jesus. Then, one day lightening struck him blind and Jesus spoke to him. (**Acts 9**) Christ came to him and demanded he go to Damascus. He did so blind and helpless, but there Saul was re-born! Saul became Paul and he was tormented by his guilt. Therefore, he traveled and was taught by Jesus. On Mt. Sani Paul made up his mind. He return and went into the church and began teaching.

Here in **Ephesians 69-18** Paul uses his prior knowledge of war to explain our Spiritual War. He uses every part of his old uniform to describe his new uniform. Paul calls us to stand. The word stand is recorded in verses: 11, 13, and 14. Thank God we do not have to stand alone. Jesus left but He sent the Holy Spirit never leaves us. Paul's shield may have been his most important part of the uniform and for us today we should never put it down. Not even to sleep!

What does the shield do physically that matches up spiritually?

_____

_____

_____

Friend, when our shields of faith operate at full capacity we are more than conquerors. What does **Romans 8:37** tell us concerning this manner?

_____

_____

_____

Scriptures instructs us that there is five types of faith.

1. One has <u>no faith</u>. (**Mark 4:40**)
2. A person with <u>little faith</u> (**Matthew 8:26 & 14:31**)
3. One can have <u>weak faith</u>. (**Romans 14:1**)
4. There is <u>strong faith</u>. (**Romans 4:20**)
5. You can have <u>great faith</u>. (**Matthew 8:10**)

(Mark 4:40) (Matthew 8:26) (Romans 4:19)
How is your faith? Which scripture matches your faith?

_____

_____

_____

If you have great faith then write a prayer of thanksgiving. If not then write a prayer of petition.

_____

_____

_____

What are these fiery darts?

_____

_____

_____

The following is a list of fiery darts in scripture.
1. Dismay—**1 Sam. 30:63**.
2. Doubt/Distrust – **2 Corinthians 4:8**

3. Skepticism—**Gen. 3:1; 1 Tim. 2:8**
4. Disruption — **Gen. 3:4-5**
5. Hopelessness — **Matt. 14:30**
6. Double-mindedness — **Matt. 6:24; Eph. 4:14; 1 John 2:15-17; James 1:8**
7. Lying – **2 Cor. 4:2**
8. Deceitfulness – **2 Thess. 2:8-12; 2 Cor. 2:17; 4:1-2**
9. Dullness — **Heb. 5:12-14; 1 Cor. 3:1-3**
10. Numbness — **Eph. 2:1-5; Romans 6:1-2; 6:11; James 2:17**
11. Falling-off — **Heb. 4:7-8; James 4:13-15**
12. Discord — **Prov. 6:16-19**
13. Corruption — **1 Cor. 3:16-17**
14. Slander — **Heb. 6:10; Matt. 10:41-42**
15. Noncompliance — **1 Sam. 15:22-23; Acts 26:12-19; Romans 6:14**

The dart was an arrow! Let's examine a war mentioned in the scripture that supports my thought. In the book of Daniel the words records the prediction of the downfall of Babylon. I find it fascinating that the following scriptures support Daniel's interpolation of a dream. Read the following scriptures and highlight the details that support Daniel's exclamation.

Jeremiah 51:11 The Lord has stirred up the spirit of the kings of the Medes, because his purpose concerning Babylon is to destroy it?

_____

_____

_____

Jeremiah 51:28 Prepare the nations for war against her, the kings of the Medes, with their governors and deputies, and every land under their dominion.
Isaiah 13:17 Behold, I am stirring up the Medes against them.
Isaiah 21:2 Go up, O Elam, lay siege, O Media

_____

_____

_____

The Median Empire

The above scriptures suggest that God would stir up the people in the land of Media against the country of Babylon. The people who were citizens of the country of Media were called Medes. However, if you read an earlier chapter, there is evidence that notes Elam would take over the nation of Babylon. The people of Persian descent lived in Elam. (**Daniel 2**) Daniel's interpreted the dream to mean that the kingdom of silver would be the Medes. The Medes would win and appoint King Darius as the new King. King Darius seems to know the of Daniel's God than did Nebuchadnezzar (**Daniel 6:16**).

Daniel 5:31

_____

_____

_____

Daniel 9:1

_____

_____

_____

Daniel 11:1

_____

_____

_____

In **Daniel 5:28 and 6:8 Daniel** reported that Babylon was conquered by Medes and Persians. Notice, that Daniel emphasizes the new king is a Mede and that the Babylonian kings were succeeded by a Median king and then by the Kings of Persia.

Lesson Side-Note:

With this next statement, I want to challenge your thought. Read it carefully and record what you think it means? Re-read the Bible prophecy found in Isaiah 13. (noted above) It's interesting that Babylon was knocked down and rebuilt several times, but we still have not seen it gone for forever. I believe the end of time is here. I further believe, that we are in the finally stage of life and the Middle East is in the news daily. The Medes or as we know them today, the Kurds, is allowing God's final judgment upon the people of Babylon. When we say Babylon today we really mean the land of Iraq. Iraq is the ancient country of Babylon. Currently, Babylonians are an independent state. The country has begun to gain power and will strike southward. Do you think that our current lesson in civics is the kind of extinction God pronounces in Isaiah 13?

Isaiah 13:17-22?

_____

_____

_____

Now let's get back to our main focus. Let's examine some weaponry. The Persian army was high in size. Partly because they possessed a large tract of land and their population was off the charts. The sheer size of the army meant that they could lose a ton of men and still win. Most of the soldiers were archers and they were considered to be the foot troops of the army. They could fire an innumerable number of arrows or javelins at a time. The _javelin_ is a spear. The arrows or javelins were long and weighted about two and a half pounds. At first, the arrow was made with a sturdy branch. The soldier, placed a sharp rock at the end of the wood. When fired, the sharp rock would stick to the shield, bruise the skin, or create a lesion on the skin. On the other hand, the Medes and Persians discovered a more effective way to kill their enemy. The soldiers created a rock that resembled a fish hook. This new fishhook would actually stick to the shield. All military forces faced their enemies by forming a line and uniting their shields. After a solider received several fish- hooked arrows, the shield would become heavy. The heaviness of the shield would make the solider unable to hold his shield correctly. The shield would begin to drop. This would create an opportunity for the last arrow to penetrate through a bodily organ resulting in death. If death was the result then the nest tow soldiers had to re connect shields, but during these moments hundreds of soldiers could fall into slumber. The goal was to stay unitied. Scripture tells us to stay united also. Consider, **1 Corinthians 6:17**, because Jesus calls us to gather (as Christian) more frequently as we see the prophecy of scripture being fulfilled. Jesus rewards us as we come in one accord. In fact, **Matthew 18:20** reveals where three are three gathered in the name of Jesus, He will be in the mist.

The shields of the Bible

A. There were 300 gold shields in the Temple (**1 Kings 10:17**).
B These were replaced by 300 shields of brass (**1 Kings 14:27**).
C The shields in the Roman times were wood covered in six layers of animal skins.

At this time in history, the people did not own leather. The soldiers quickly had to develop a plan to repeal the darts of the enemy. They developed a new use for animal skins, because they were readily available. The military hollowed-out trees and wrapped the shield in saturated animal skins. The soldiers then developed a hook which would penetrated through the shield quickly. This caused a deadly problem for their enemies. The military leaders decided to saturate or anoint the animal skins with oil. Then, they wrapped their shields and their forearm with the anointed animal skins.

I wonder what type of oil was used?

I do not think it was an expensive oil! That rules out the anointing oil, frankincense, and myrrh. I believe that the army used a simple carrier oil. Today, we use fractionated coconut oil, but at this time in history olive oil or vegetable oil would have been available and inexpensive.

What do you know about the word anoint?

_____

_____

_____

What is the dictionary definition of the word anointing?

_____

_____

_____

According to bing.com Powered by Oxford Dictionaries · © Oxford University Press

Anointing means the following:

1. smear or rub with oil, typically as part of a religious ceremony: "high priests were anointed with oil" · "bodies were anointed after death for burial"

2. (anoint something with) smear or rub something with (any other substance): "Cuna Indians anoint the tips of their arrows with poison"

3. ceremonially confer divine or holy office

Psalms 133:2

_____

_____

_____

Isiah 21:5

_____

_____

_____

In the book of Psalms, the psalmist uses Aaron's example of anointment. This psalmist stated to take precious oil and do what with it?

Look back at the lesson on oil. Why was oil precious to the Children of God?

_____

_____

_____

The Jews had many customs in which they used essential oils. The essential oils were created by God for His people to use as medicine. The essential oils were used in every aspect of the Jewish lifestyle. For example, essential oils were used to cleanse, heal, and protect the Jews. In the scripture of **Psalm 133:2** the psalmist recommends anointing their entire shield. This anointment is like the precious ointment upon the head, that ran down upon the beard, and even to the garments; therefore, we are to anoint their bodies from top to bottom. For example, the Medes soldier would make sure that every inch of his shield was saturated with oil! This means each soldier prayed 6 times, because their were six layers of animal skin. Anointing the shield took time, care, and discipline. The anointing of the shield is our modern-day comparison to having the Holy Spirit all over you! In ancient times, the anointed shields of the solders deflected the enemies fish-hooked darts and the oil deflected the sun. Today, the Holy Spirit deflects the darts of Satan and illuminates the son. Finally, both of the results created a positive result for the Roman army as well as God's army. The army could save the lives of more men and win the war.

Today, when you have anointed from top to bottom you have become more defensive and you are able to withstand the wiles of the devil. The holy anointing allows us to speak boldly, fight the enemy, live uprightly, and obey God. We must perform the duties of a solider in God's army! We must anoint our shields of faith daily! Remember, Paul's message does not teach us to mirror the image of a Roman soldier, but to instead resemble a soldier bound for enteral life.

Later on the time line, men of war used leather to cover their shields. The solider had to kept the leather layers of his shield supple.

What does it mean to keep the layers of leather supple?

_____

_____

_____

This means to use oil and lubricate your shield. Romans oiled their shields every morning. They would have used olive oil or after the men slaughtered cattle, the lower leg bones were tossed to the side, and then boiled to get the brine. An oil that we call Neatsfoot oil was then created. This is a yellow oil rendered and purified from the shin bones and feet (but not the hooves) of cattle. "Neat" in the oil's name comes from an old English word for cattle. 2,000 years ago Neatsfoot oil was used to anoint each soldiers shields. Today, neatfoot oil is used to conditioning, softening, and preservative leather.

Therefore scripture tell us to keep our shields oiled up. If not, dry shield produce cracks. When a dart of fire hit a dry shield, the shield would explode into fire. Who wants to get burned?

_____

_____

_____

How did they treat a burn victim?

_____

_____

_____

Burn treatments used by the Romans and Jews were simple. A burn was a burn and there was no such identification; such as a first, second, or third degree burn. Modern medicine instructs to seal and moisturized each burn.

1. First room temperature water was applied. (Not cold because they did not use refrigeration).
2. God's people did have access to many types of animal eggs, but today we would grab chicken eggs. They used (and even today) egg whites to coat the burns. To do this grab two eggs, scramble them,

and use a cloth or basting brush to coat the burn. Using clean cotton rags coat one side and tie around the burn.

3. Some people converted axle grease (which was made of animal fat and beeswax) and combined turpentine to clean the burn.
4. Strong tea was placed directly on the burn as an overnight treatment.
5. Clean fabric was made into a tea-sized sack and filled with cow manure and placed on burn overnight.
6. Blisters were not broke because this would have released the infection.
7. Pure wild honey coated the burn to seal it for rapid healing.
8. Petroleum accurately depicts oil that is found under rock. Jews used this to cover the bodies of people who were badly burned.

Side Note: The petroleum industry was reported by archaeolgists as coming from a village named Hit. This village was located on the banks of the Euphrates river in Iraq. Today, archaeologists call this seeping of oil The Fountains Of Pitch. 6000 years ago that's 4,000 years before Jesus the people used this sticky oil as mortar between rocks. I guess today, we call this Asphalt. So, they would have used this (asphalt) as waterproofing. Their town baths, pottery, baskets, and water crafts were leak proof because of this agent. For example, The Babylonians caulked their ships in Mesopotamia with this asphalt. (4000 B.C.) The walls of Babylon and the the pyramids could have also been sealed with this oil. Egyptians used it for embalming. The Romans may have called this bitumen, because a biblical scholar sited it as being used to coat Moses' basket and provided evidence that Noah's Ark was coated with it from top to bottom. Later, the American Indians used it to light their lamps, glue their yarn, and seal their arrowheads.

9. Lavender Oil and Coconut Oil for Burns: Lavender essential oil has numerous health benefits that were discovered more than 2000 years ago.
10. Frankincense can reduce scaring.
11. Melaleuca decrease infection especially after popping a blister.
12. Peppermint to provide pain management.

Did a burn victim usually survive?

_____

_____

_____

The answer lies deep into what type of burn and what the Jews could actually get from their environment. The Bible records several being burned up and talks about the consuming fire a great deal. I believe a small burn that we get today could easily kill someone that lived two-thousand years ago.

Therefore, all solders knew the risks and kept his shield oily and slick. Oftentimes, he would drench his shield into the water. What does this picture represent to you?

_____

_____

_____

To lead your thoughts, consider the following verses of scriptures!

Exodus 17:6

_____

_____

_____

1 Corinthians 10:4

_____

_____

_____

The word water is being used as a symbol to refer to the Word of God. The Word of God is our Bible. According to **Exodus 17:6** the citizens of Israel drank water, in the wilderness, from a rock. According to 1 Corinthians the rock directly pointed to Jesus.

Exodus 17:6 Behold, I will stand before you there on the rock in Horeb; and you shall strike the rock, and water will come out of it, that the people may drink." And Moses did so in the sight of the elders of Israel.

1 Corinthians 10:4 and all drank the same spiritual drink. For they drank of that spiritual Rock that followed them, and that Rock was Christ.

Recap:

What did you learn from this lesson?

_____

_____

_____

The goal of this lesson was to give you a deeper understanding of scripture. One of the most important things to remember is that we are not permitted to allow our shield to become dry. A dry shield generates cracks and then anything could pass threw and kill the soldiers. Satan's fiery darts will ignite and destroy your faith. You can't fight with a dry shield! So, don't let your faith become dry! You must have an anointing of the Holy Ghost to survive and fill God's purpose for your life! Dry shields can't connect or unite to make anointed Churches. Dry Churches can't produce anointed soldiers! Soldiers of the army keep your shields soft, slick, and oily. Always be ready to be called into battle. Today, we need to be ready for spiritual battle. I hope you understand the importance of the shield of faith. I pray that God continues to give you favor and protection from this world and all its enemies.

SLEEP IS A GIFT

CLASS SCRIPT

According to en.wikipedia.org/wiki/Sleep: "**Sleep** is a naturally recurring state of mind characterized by altered consciousness, relatively inhibited sensory activity, inhibition of nearly all voluntary muscles, and reduced interactions with surroundings. It is distinguished from wakefulness by a decreased ability to react to stimuli, but is more easily reversed than the state of hibernation or of being comatose."

Healthy sleep is imperative to our physical and mental health. I find it difficult to identify healthy sleep patterns when just examining my pattern compared to those around me. According to my doctor adults should sleep seven to nine hours; however, the sleep needs of people are different! For example, I feel my best when I can sleep a full eight hours, but I find I only get about five hours and I must nap during the day. I notice in my children and myself that if our sleep schedule changes we are in for an intolerable day!

How is your sleep pattern?

_____

_____

_____

According to a survey conducted by Consumer Reports Magazine Forty-four percent of Americans have issues with sleeping. Some sleepers, experience difficulty falling asleep, staying asleep, and often wake up too early. This pretty matches my life! How do you sleep?

_____

_____

_____

How does the lack of sleep interfere with our lives?

_____

_____

_____

When we are, sleep deprived our body and mind is affected. Below are some examples of what sleep deprivation causes. If you can think of a concrete answer be sure to write it down and share with your study group. If you don't have a study group share the book, the question, and answer on Facebook. You are sure to receive some great reactions.

1. The loss of sleep is public safety hazard! (Hint for the teacher: be sure to discuss that sleep deprivation is as dangerous as drunk driving.)

    _____

    _____

    _____

2. How about the fatigue at work? Could it cause accidents? Yes, work compensation studies have done and report the lack of sleep causes accidents that result in being off work longer than just being sick.

    _____

    _____

    _____

3. the lack of sleep also affects your memory and ability to learn. Think about your attention span, alertness, concentration, reasoning, and problem solving.

    _____

    _____

    _____

4. According to the *Journal of Clinical Endocrinology & Metabolism* (in 2002) reports that several men develop sleep apnea also have low testosterone levels.

_____

_____

_____

5. Sleep deprivation also cause depression and anxiety symptoms to worsen. In some people, it causes nervousness and aggression. (Note for the teacher: you may consider discussing road rage and introduce lavender because of their calming ability. Below are some oils you should have for this lesson. While discussing them pass around the valve so your class/guests can experience. It's also nice to defuse them during class. Be sure to point out this is probably has caused yawning in group.) The number of cases for people seeking medical advice for a sleep disorders have increased, almost doubled, in the last decade.

I will admit that I am in the number of people who have sleeping dilemmas. I wholeheartedly blame these disorders on my brain trauma. My sleeping disorder is so severe that it interferes with everything including my physical and mental abilities during the day. In addition, sleep depravity also causes, relationship conflicts, impairs good judgement, makes me easily distractible, and irritable.

So, what's God's Medicine? Well, believe it or not When God made the vegetation of the world He made different plants that have helped increased my sleep. For example, almonds and walnuts are two of the best nuts you can eat right before bed. That's because eating walnuts causes the human brain to secrete melatonin. My body sure lacks melatonin. More than one doctor has told me. Melatonin is the chemical responsible for regulating the body's internal clock. On the other hand, researchers have described walnuts as containing enough melatonin to impact struggling sleeplessness. Finally, it takes at least an hour for melatonin levels to elevate after you've eaten, I have my snack at 6:00 p.m. - my scheduled bedtime.

Oatmeal is an incredible food and I actually like the healthy kind. Not only as one of the foods that help me sleep, but current research suggests that weight loss and cholesterol will decrease. Oats contain both magnesium and calcium. On the other hand, I wish Oatmeal cookies would give me the same result! Finally, most carbohydrates, along with tryptophan containing foods help me stay asleep longer. However, this is not recommended for people overweight people like me.

Two minerals that increase sleep are magnesium and calcium. I wish I was the only one deficient in both of these nutrients, but. Unfortunately, these minerals are the most common ones that the human body system is lacking. Magnesium has a calming effect on the body and is also an important building block for melatonin. A deficiency of magnesium can be one of the causes of insomnia.

One of my dietitians suggested snacking on dried fruit. I got excited that day, because I do like dried fruits, but these are the ones that she suggested: prunes, raisins, peaches, apricots, and dates. Next, she suggested I increase my intake of Tomatoes, potatoes, carrots, radishes and garlic. Then, at the end of our counseling session she gives me a paper to mark off all of my Leafy greens, for the week. I can't say a marked off there are mini of the following: green beets, spinach, turnip greens and Swiss chard. These are great power food from God, because they provide magnesium, calcium and potassium, but I guess I'll have to ask him to give me the taste buds for those examples.

The Written word yes God makes me lie down. (Psalm32:2) read the following passages and paraphrase what you learned on the lines below.

Ecc 5:12

_____

_____

_____

The sleep of a laboring man is sweet, whether he eat little or much: but the abundance of the rich will not suffer him to sleep.

After presenting the information that the Holy Spirit guided me to about this is an important scripture. First it tells us that we must labor, it doesn't matter if we eat a little or a lot, God caused the man to sleep.

Psalm 16:9

_____

_____

_____

God is always watching over you and me.

1. **Psalm 121:2-5** My help comes from the Lord, the maker of heaven and earth. He will not let you fall. Your guardian will not fall asleep. Indeed, the Guardian of Israel never rests or sleeps. The Lord is your guardian. The Lord is the shade over your right hand.

   _____

   _____

   _____

2. **Proverbs 3:24** When you lie down, you will not be afraid. When you rest, your sleep will be peaceful.

   _____

   _____

   _____

3. **Psalm 4:7-8** But you have made me happier than they will ever be with all their wine and grain. When I go to bed, I sleep in peace, because, Lord, you keep me safe.

   _____

   _____

   _____

4. **Psalm 3:3-6** But you, Lord, protect me. You bring me honor; you give me hope. I will pray to the Lord, and he will answer me from his holy mountain. I can lie down to rest and know that I will wake up, because the Lord covers and protects me. So, I will not be afraid of my enemies, even if thousands of them surround me.

   _____

   _____

   _____

I hope if you are a person that does not sleep well you are comforted in those words. At night I quote my favorite scripture in nighttime prayers.

However, my snooze routine also involves a number of other steps. First, at about 6 o'clock I have a serving of almonds, walnuts, and a banana. About a half an hour later I'll take a warm bath with a mixture of lavender, vetiver, yland gland, and Roman chamomile. Next, I take a veggie cap with those oils inside. Finally, I use my diffuser which runs about four hours.

1. I have found that **Lavender oil** helps me to relax, eases my stress, and more. Lavender has properties make are even gentle enough to use on your dogs, horses, and cats.
2. In Germany, the root from **Valerian** roots are distilled and great for relaxing.
3. **Vetiver** oil is well known for its grounding and calming agents. Some people have reported to me that this oil helped them recover from trauma.
4. About every night I defuse **Roman Chamomile.** Did you know in Ancient Egypt, Chamomile was dedicated to the sun god, Ra? Ra was evoked to restore wholeness to the Self. When I have mixed this oil for message it has helped me relax and clear my thoughts.
5. **Marjoram** Oil is high in antioxidants! After a long day, I message this oil directly into my skin. I've even done this while saying my nightly prayers. Scientist belief this to affect the nervous systems and helps us to sleep, because it calms down our active nerves.

_____

_____

_____

Now that we understand our topic for this class let's consultant God's word. I have generated a list of scriptures below. I would like for you to analyze each one and highlight the ones that address our topic.

Additional Bible Verses About Sleep

Bible verses related to *Sleep* from the King James Version (KJV)

Proverbs 20:13 - Love not sleep, lest thou come to poverty; open thine eyes, [and] thou shalt be satisfied with bread.

Proverbs 6:9 - How long wilt thou sleep, O sluggard? when wilt thou arise out of thy sleep?

Psalms 132:4 - 127:5 - I will not give sleep to mine eyes, [or] slumber to mine eyelids,

Psalms 91:1-16 - He that dwelleth in the secret place of the most High shall abide under the shadow of the Almighty.

Matthew 8:24 - And, behold, there arose a great tempest in the sea, insomuch that the ship was covered with the waves: but he was asleep.

Have you ever considered sleep as a gift?

_____

_____

_____

We should receive sleep with thanksgiving and gratitude. If we are not getting enough sleep, we need to question why. As we learned above sleep affects just about everything in our lives. Some people have medical reasons that they do not get enough sleep, but some people get up to early and go the bed too late. Does this describe you or someone you know? Explain the situation:

_____

_____

_____

My restless night's sleep is somewhat caused by the side effects from brain surgery. On the other hand, some people believe they need more money. They need to obtain Earthly treasures to be happy. While others stay up late poisoning their minds with inappropriate movies. Sometimes, we think our work and wants are important, but the Psalm above clearly states that sleep is a gift. Therefore, refusing sleep is similar to telling God that our work is more important than His. What work do you think God completes when he allows our bodies to sleep?

_____

_____

_____

Below I have a few suggestions to help you sleep. If you do not need the information below why not share it with someone struggling. For what's it is worth, I've tested each recommendation. May God bless you with this special gift.

1. In prayer, ask God to give you restful sleep!
2. Try the Essential Oils I mentioned and I'm sure you'll have a better night sleep.

SOAP

CLASS SCRIPT

(See: video on YouTube)

Introduction Questions:

What is Soap?

_____

_____

_____

    The scientific method used to describe how soap is crafted is called saponification. Basically, soap is produced by combining animal fats and salt; thus, generating acids. Then, the Israelites created glycerin. To prepare animal fat for rendering one must: Remove all skin, muscle, ligaments, tendons and meat to leave only animal fat, commonly referred to as tallow. (Any animal fat can be used, but beef fat is most commonly used).

    Next, the Israelites cut the tallow into small pieces and melt the tallow over a low flame on the stove in a pot. Irrevocably, to preserve soap, Old Testament saints stored the two mixtures separately.

Why do we use soap?

_____

_____

_____

What brand of soap does your family use?

_____

_____

_____

In the Old Testament how did God's Children keep clean

_____

_____

_____

One of the most primitive incidents of the Bible was when Cain became a tiller of the soil and his brother Abel became a keeper of the flock (Genesis 4:2). Later in Hebrew history, the herds of sheep and goats roamed the same paddock. Both herds of animals were consumed for milk and meat. The skin of the animals was recycled into fabrics. The textiles were worn as clothing, but they also used them as rugs and as canopies. Recover the following scriptures for further discovery.

Isaiah 7:21-22

_____

_____

_____

Proverbs 27:27

_____

_____

_____

Deuteronomy 14:4

_____

_____

_____

Leviticus 13:47

_____

_____

_____

Exodus 25:4

_____

_____

_____

The goat's skin provided bottles in to store liquids and essential oils. The uncut hide of either animal might have been the wineskin of Jesus' parables. You can locate the following scriptures for further discovery. While investigating, note if you think the uncut hide was considered wineskin?

Mark 2:22

_____

_____

_____

Matthew 9:17

_____

_____

_____

Luke 5:37-38

_____

_____

_____

"Cleanliness is next to Godliness"

Science has gained momentum over the last 35 centuries. Scientist discovered a germ in 1880. Handwashing was not practiced as well as it should have been in the hospital. I remember my grandma divulging that her family did not go to the hospital, because she claimed that you came out sicker than you were when you came to the hospital. For example, when her mother was giving birth to a sibling she almost died, because double contamination occurred. double contamination occurred when doctors treated one patient, did not wash their hands, and then treated another patient. According to scripture, God people to be clean. God knew the importance of being clean and new were problems with the car if his people were not clean.

In the Word of God, we find several passages references we can infer that God values aromatic plants, trees, herbs in association to bathing, washing, cleansing or purification. Scripture also reports the idea of "Cleanliness is next to Godliness," but the words are not written in that exact language. This is actually an old saying that still corresponds in today's culture. This ancient proverb is known to derive from ancient Hebrew writings; however, the true origin of this saying can be inferred from biblical scriptures. There are over one hundred passages indicating we should be clean in our body and in the condition of our heart. Examining this topic in scripture, please locate, read, and paraphrase **2 Corinthians 7:1**.

_____

_____

_____

The Greek word translated means "godliness;" however, in the New Testament we read: "holiness." Again, without which no one will see God who is not clean (**Hebrews 12:14**). Is holiness obtained by keeping the Law? No, it is impossible! Read the evidence in (**Romans 3:20 and Galatians 2:16**). More over when the blood is applied Christ makes us a new creation. Explore this topic more by investing these two passages: **2 Corinthians 5:17; Ephesians 4:24**.

_____

_____

_____

*IF YOU WERE UNCLEAN WHAT WERE THE STIPULATIONS?

In the Old Testament God established contamination routines, cleanliness regiments, and an entirely different system for armies. For example, in Leviticus and Exodus scripture documents that people were quarantined for encountering dead animals or people and more.

Numbers 31:19

"And you, camp outside the camp seven days; whoever has killed any person and whoever has touched any slain, purify yourselves, you and your captives, on the third day and on the seventh day.

In the following scriptures note the practice in the space provided.

Numbers 19:11

_____

_____

_____

Exodus 19:10

_____

_____

_____

2 Kings 15:5

The LORD struck the king, so that he was a leper to the day of his death And he lived in a separate house, while Jotham the king's son was over the household, judging the people of the land.

Numbers 5:2

"Command the sons of Israel that they send away from the camp every leper and everyone having a discharge and everyone who is unclean because of a dead person.

A Levite, which was like a preacher, also was utilized as being the town's doctor. The Levite priest, was the only one allowed to enter the quarantine and treat the patients. After returning from the quarantine God demanded that he wash his clothes three times and put his clothes in the sunlight for seven days. This was a purification ritual that protected the people from spreading diseases hand illnesses. The following scriptures describe what happened if a person became clean.

Leviticus 13:6

_____

_____

_____

Numbers 31:24

_____

_____

_____

Numbers 12:14-15

But the LORD said to Moses, "If her father had but spit in her face, would she not bear her shame for seven days? Let her be shut up for seven days outside the camp, and afterward she may be received again." So Miriam was shut up outside the camp for seven days, and the people did not move on until Miriam was received again.

Men:

Leviticus 13:45-46

"As for the leper who has the infection, his clothes shall be torn, and the hair of his head shall be uncovered, and he shall cover his mustache and cry, 'Unclean! Unclean!'

Women:

Leviticus 15:19

"When a woman has a discharge, if her discharge in her body is blood, she shall continue in her menstrual impurity for seven days; and whoever touches her shall be unclean until evening.

Deuteronomy 23:10-11

Check out these two version?

1. **NIV** "If there is among you any man who is unclean because of a <u>nocturnal emission</u>, then he must go outside the camp; he may not reenter the camp.
2. **KJV** "If there is any man among you who becomes unclean by some occurrence in the night, then he shall go outside the camp; he shall not come inside the camp. 11 But it shall be, when evening comes, that he shall wash with water; and when the sun sets, he may come into the camp."

What is **nocturnal emission**?

_____

_____

_____

"Holy Smoke!" Can you believe that definition! According to King James this scripture is discussing the principle of burying filth; such as, dung, manure, dirt, and feces was given by the Scriptures over 1400. God told Moses and the children of Israel: "Thou shalt have a place also. without the camp, whither thou shalt go forth abroad: and thou shalt have a paddle upon thy weapon; and it shall be, when thou wilt ease thyself abroad, thou shalt dig therewith, and shalt turn back and cover that which cometh from thee" (**Deut. 23:12-13**).

Regrettably, in our current world the public has lost sight of the fundamentals of sanitation. Therefore, preventing disease has become problematic. Our leading cities have increasingly become congested, polluted, filthy and dirty. Our landfills are filled to the brim with garbage. The quality of the air is unfit to breathe, because of contaminates from industrial chemicals, municipal wastes, and gas omissions from automobiles. Sin has a consequence! Could our actions of violating Bible principles be the underwriting cause to why contagious diseases are escalating?

_____

_____

_____

The Biblical commandments for disinfecting, personal hygiene, and purification were not purely duties and rituals. These demands were God's safeguards for Israel. The safeguards decreased health hazards, contagious diseases, and deadly epidemics!

In the Old Testament God set up content contaminated routines, cleanliness regiments, and entirely different system for armies.

Numbers 19:11 (3 types)

_____

_____

_____

Exodus 19:10

_____

_____

_____

A Levite, which was like a preacher, also was utilized as being the town's doctor. The Levite priest, was the only one allowed to enter the quarantine and treat the patients. After returning from the quarantine God demanded that he wash his clothes and himself three times and put his clothes in the sunlight for seven days. This was a purification ritual that protected the people from spreading diseases hand illnesses.

Leviticus 13:6

_____

_____

_____

Numbers 31:24

_____

_____

_____

Scriptures of being cleaned with hyssop are as follows: (Highlight the essential oils mentioned in the passages.)

Numbers 19:17-20

'Then for the unclean person they shall take some of the ashes of the burnt purification from sin and flowing water shall be added to them in a vessel.

1 Kings 4:33

He spoke of trees, from the cedar that is in Lebanon even to the hyssop that grows on the wall; he spoke also of animals and birds and creeping things and fish.

Exodus 12:22

"You shall take a bunch of hyssop and dip it in the blood which is in the basin and apply some of the blood that is in the basin to the lintel and the two doorposts; and none of you shall go outside the door of his house until morning.

PLEASE READ PSALM 51:7 AND DETERMINE HOW THE WORDS RELATE TO OUR THEME.

The book of Psalm is the most beneficial and researched book of the Bible. The words provide advice on everything that mankind faces today. The oaths in Psalm interpretants the birth of Jesus to the last scenes of Christ death on that dreadful cross. King David verified that our Eternal God bestowed him with many gifts and blessings within his written expression. For example, **Psalm 51:7** he declares, "Purge me with hyssop, and I shall be clean; wash me, and I shall be whiter than snow." David's words speak to a spiritual washing. David is blatantly requesting for God to give him a supernatural cleansing. Through this passage we've determined only the Almighty God can make a mankind clean and pure. Even if our sins have covered us in filth.

Side Note (Reminder) Scriptural reference 2 Samuel 11:3,

The sin of David began simply, because it commenced with him choosing to stay in Jerusalem; while, he sends the rest of the Israelite army into battle. The first scene of David's vacation draws us into the sighting of David relaxing on the rooftop of the palace. From his fabulous view he catches a glimpse of a beautiful woman. David immediately sends men to find out all they can about this woman. When they return, with their retrieved information, they are very clear about her identity. The servants informed the kind that her name was Bathsheba, the daughter of Eliam and the wife of Uriah. His next action, plunges him directly into sin of the worse type -sexual sin. His sends his men to fetch her and then he rapes her. After some time as past (the Bible does not specifically give a time frame) Bathsheba later send word to David that she was pregnant.

David was panicky, because he did not want his sin to find him out. Therefore, the King called for Uriah to come back to Jerusalem from the war. He thought he could persuade Uriah to sleep with his wife; thus, covering up his sin. This sad event ends in the death of Uriah but brings us into David's plasm of repentance. The prophet Nathan visited King David and told him of the Lord's disapproval and displeasure with David. Even though David repented of his sin, Nathan told David that the son Bathsheba was expecting would die.

Sin can be expressed in the symbolism of the following expression: "If you stay around a pig pin, then you are likely to get a little on you." Sin can often be skin deep! Sometimes, we wear the shield of guilt! In my mind's eye, in this illustration; I can clearly see white clothing blotted with dirt and grime and that is to say the least. My family has been blessed with a hobby farm and pigs are my favorite; therefore, by experience God has explained this quote to me physically.

Side Note 2 (out of pure curiosity let's investigate)

Turn to **1 Chronicles 3.5** The relationship between Bathsheba and King David did not begin well, but she later became his loyal wife and mother of King Solomon, the wisest ruler of Israel. Her life experience is document in the following sentences: **2 Samuel 11:1-3, 12:24; 1 Kings 1:11-31, 2:13-19; 1 Chronicles 3:5; Psalm 51:1.**

Bathsheba was a member of the upper-class society. Her father was a righteous man and taught Bathsheba about all the laws God had created for them. He was present and even blessed her union to Uriah. Eliam was also a great warrior and well-known for victories among the people. Therefore, when David's sin found him out that he lost the rule of the kingdom. Our sin is always forgiven, but we still have to pay the consequences.

Family Tree:

Father - Eliam
Husbands - Uriah the Hittite, and King David.
Sons - An unnamed son (1st born & Died), <u>King Solomon</u>, Shammua, Shobab, and Nathan.

When we say, "snow-white" we consider that to be the definitive of whites. David's expression "I shall be whiter than snow." Proclaims that God granted him absolute spiritual cleanness which imputes a state of perfect holiness. At the commencement of section 7, David intentionally invites God to purge him with hyssop. Hyssop is a motivating cleansing agent, and he knew the Old Testament and understood this (**Exodus 12:22**.) The hyssop branch is an herb. This type of herb is included in the mint family. It's often referred to a species of marjoram. The hyssop plant reaches a height of only three feet tall. The plants aroma came from the bundles of variously colored flowers. During ancient times, God planted hyssop in between rocky crevices. God's beloved removed the full branches and blooms from their balcony walls. Fresh hyssop was most commonly used; however, dried flowers made hair pieces and jewelry.

According to the Old Testament, these bunches were used for ritual purposes. The general routines of hyssop being depleted spiritually were logged in **Exodus 12:22**. Hyssop had an impact at all Passover celebrations. For example, Moses instructed the people to take a bunch of hyssop, dip it in the blood of the basin, and paint the mixture on the lintel and the two doorposts. God's people knew hyssop's spiritual lessons, because the information was passed-down from previous generations. For example, in the books of the law (Leviticus and Numbers), hyssop was used as the nucleus in the service. In the church tent hyssop was tied into bunches and used like a broom; to dust the blood of animal and even scattering the blood onto the Israelites.

A more clearer use age of hyssop is evident **In Numbers 19**. Here, Moses gives advises his people that God has declared any person who touches an unclean animal must perform a cleansing ritual. The instructions for this time of cleansing included; seizing the collected hyssop, tying it; and drying it for 3 days, plunging it into clean flowing water; and sprinkling the unclean person, his shelter, and belongings. This example, obviously links hyssop and clean water as a form of soap. Furthermore, this process signified a separation and a protection for God's children versus the deadly destruction that God would bring on the Egyptians. Moreover, God cleansed and protected His people both privately in their lodgings and against the plague of the death of the Egyptians first born animals and children, because of

Pharaoh's disobedience, the unfair treatment of His beloved, and for their repugnance of ungodliness.

Next, Moses advised the people to remain in their dwellings until morning has passed. The Israelites were to sustain from the Egyptians and even called for a strike from work. For one day and night all interactions and communications were to be cut-off! Their lives were at stake and the Bible points out that all Israelites meet God's commands.

Historical records declare that hyssop contains antiseptic, sterile, and germ-killing cleansing assets. Remember that would "disinfect" what scripture does that match? (hint: To disinfect the contaminated person or his possessions?)

Examples:

a. 2 Corinthians 7:1 ESV
Since we have these promises, beloved, let us cleanse
ourselves from every defilement of body and spirit,
bringing holiness to completion in the fear of God.

b. 1 Corinthians 6:19 ESV
Or do you not know that your body is a temple of the
Holy Spirit within you, whom you have from God?

So, what does hyssop represent biblically?

_____

_____

_____

The point is not about how the essential oil is beneficial, but it's the fact the Jesus is our only source for total purification. All the sacrifices and ceremonies in the Old Testament about cleansings was and is a continuous notice that these events capture the designed picture of how Jesus is the only washing, cleansing, restoring, and purification that grants us salvation. It's this salvation that defeats the enemy of death and is the key to everlasting life. In this Psalm, David delivers his message of being purged with hyssop.

THE RED HEIFER

A more clearer use age of hyssop is evident In Numbers 19. Here, Moses advises his people that God has declared any person who touches an unclean animal; though, they must perform a cleansing ritual. The instructions for this type of cleansing included; seizing the collected hyssop, tying it; and drying it for 3 days, plunging it into clean flowing water; and sprinkling the unclean person, his shelter, and belongings. This example, scripture obviously links hyssop and clean water as a form of soap. Furthermore, this process signified a separation and a protection for God's children versus the deadly destruction that God would bring on the Egyptians. Moreover, God cleansed and protected His people both privately in their lodgings and against the plague of the death that the Egyptians faced with their first-born animals and children, because of Pharaoh's disobedience, the unfair treatment of His beloved, and for their repugnance of ungodliness.

The focus of this simple lesson comes from Numbers 19:1-22 (And the LORD spake unto Moses and unto Aaron, saying,) Please read the chapter 19 in its entirety.

Significance of the ashes of the Red Heifer!

Verse 3: God demanded his children to burn
the unyoked Heifer outside the camp.
Verse 4: To purifying the altar and temple of God.
Verse 5: To purifying the priest.
Verse 9: A purified man must clean up all the ashes, store t them
in a clean place, and keep them for the use of the congregation.

In **Numbers 19:11-12** the ashes of the cow were used to purify the defilements of the people. God also choose three elements of nature that served as the kindling. Read **Numbers 19:6** and record the three materials.

_____

_____

_____

The Process:

First, the heifer was selected. Then, when it was going to be sacrificed, it was lead outside the city gates to be killed. In addition, according to the scripture of **Numbers 19:3** They then gave her to Eleazar the priest. Eleazar then lead the cow outside the camp, were someone slaughtered her in his sight.

Pleas re-read Numbers 19:5. How does the burning of the cow predict the image of Jesus Christ's death on the cross?

_____

_____

_____

First of all, the passage in Numbers chapter 19:5, "And one shall burn the heifer in his sight; her skin and her blood and her flesh, with her dung, shall he burn," represents the consuming fire that only Christ can save us from entering. This event is a representation of the Messiah's death and suffering. This suffering incident is symbolized in **Isaiah 53:1-12.** Overall, these words verify that the Lord Jesus was consumed through suffering and death.

The process of the red heifer also directly links to the reference of **Hebrew 13:12**, "Wherefore Jesus also, that he might sanctify his people with his own blood, suffered outside the city." Then according to **Matthew 27:32** Jesus was also lead out of town to Golgotha. The two scriptures we just studied provide magnificent verification that the Messiah was our perfect sacrifice; and the red heifer and Passover lamb were both predictions of this event.

I love how the holy spirit teaches us how His word connects and by using this method of studying we receive the entire picture. It amazes me to understand the patterns of our topic. For instance, the cedar wood signifies the cross for which our Messiah was scorched on the Roman cross as the burnt offering. (The cross was made of cedarwood **John 19: 22-23.**) Similarly, just as Eleazar had pitched the cedar-wood in the heart of the heifer's fire, **Matthew 27:32** affirms, "And as they were going out, they found a man of Cyrene, whose name was Simon, whom they compelled to carry his cross."

The hyssop that Eleazar put in the heifer's fire reminds of what John asserted in 19:28. John wrote that Jesus remarked, "I thirst! However, **Matthew 27:34**, proclaims: "And they gave him to drink vinegar mixed with gall; and he tasted it, but he would not drink." Hyssop pinpoints the bitterness that our Messiah impacts. God hates our sin and it is revolting in His sight. The repenting of our sin was nailed to the cross as it was devoured the body of our Messiah. This very action is how the lamb and heifer exposed that Jesus is the Messiah and He became our burnt offering. Now, He sets at the right hand of the Father making intercessions for our sin. He is soon to return! Let's be ready!

The book of Numbers encompasses evidence on how impure person was made whole. (Numbers 19). The decrees of God declared that if a person came in contact with the dead that person was ceremonially unclean. This law is generated from the following scriptures: **Genesis 2:17, Deuteronomy 30:15, and Romans 6:23,** because our physical death is associated with our spiritual death. All life was deemed as religious and as a result they were bound up by symbolism and decrees. For example, **2Kings 5:15,** Examines the story of Naaman's disease. Once, Naaman was healed he recognized that there is only one God of Israel.

For the reasons of purification, the community had to sacrifice a red heifer without imperfection or fault that had never been worked. The priest detached the skin from the animal, because that signified the death of sin. The red hair of the heifer exemplified the blood of Jesus. The crucifixion of the red heifer accomplished the sacred role of foreshadowing Jesus is crucifixion.

Let's trace the steps in Israel's daily sacrifices please reference **Exodus 29:19-41.** In this section of scripture, we find an outline for five ceremonies, but first consider that all the priests had to be concentrated for Service first. Aaron was anointed with the oil on his head which symbolized his appointment of office by God, he had to be in priestly garments, and his four sons had to be dressed in their priestly garments.

Bull	Lamb	Ram	Goat
(Offered with Bread, Wavers, and Cakes Signified that Jesus had taken the place of man. He did so on the cross. He was the sacrifice!	Pinpointed to God's only Son being the Perfect Sacrifice.	Right Ear -Hearing the Word Of God. Thumb- Our mind set on Jesus. Big Toe- What service can we do for the Kingdom of God.	_____ _____ _____ _____

The first sacrifice ordered by God was a bull with bread, wafers, and cakes. This sacrifice signified that the dead bull took their place. Secondly, this sacrifice consisted of burning a lamb on the altar. The lamb resembled the occurrence of Jesus's death on the cross. The third, offering was that of a ram. This sacrifice was ordered to be placed in specific locations. For example, the placement of the blood on the right ear, represented the people hearing God's word. Possibly, the placement of blood on the thumb symbolized the holiness it takes to serve God. On the other hand, by placing a drop of cedarwood on the thumb, while studying, this improves your ability to focus and comprehended the material. Finally, the blood of the ram was placed on the big toe to symbolize walking in the will of God and sustaining from defilements. Moreover, Cedar-wood oil is a good for the feet, because it's an antiseptic and this helps improve conditions like Athlete's Foot.

The third sacrifice was to concentrate the priests for service. This was done with a bull. It was burnt every seven days and offered for the sins of the priest. The Priest had to be cleansed before each offering. Therefore, the priest had to perform the cleansing ceremony (twice a day) on the seventh day. The bull was also burned twice. Once, in the morning and once in the evening.

As if that was not enough sacrifices, the fourth was the burning of two lambs. Burning one in the morning and one in the evening. Each time a grain offering of flour and oil was consumed. Next, the priest also had a drink offering which was most likely juice. Hence, combining the offering of flour, oil, and juice represented the daily lives of the people. This sacrifice was similar to the reason Christ offered himself as a sacrifice to God. Thus, both sacrifices were pleasing to God. (**Ephesians 5:2**)

In verses three through eight, we will find that the priest slaughtered the cow outside the camp to symbolize the removal of the sin from the people. The priest then sprinkled some of the blood seven times in front of the tabernacle. Sprinkling the blood in front of the tabernacle was an offering to the Lord. Next, the priest would totally burn the cow in open flames of fire. The kindling for the fire was made of cedarwood, hyssop, and scarlet wool. All three of these materials were used in several rituals of purification. These three materials were used to purify leprosy; which, is found in Leviticus 14. Cedar wood was chosen because it is an evergreen and it's aromatic. For example, cedarwood oil prevents wounds from becoming septic and can also be used to cure diarrhea, by tightening the muscles of the digestive system and contracting those spasm-prone muscles. In addition, cedar wood purges a cough by destroying phlegm. The phlegm blocks the lungs; thus, triggering congestion. The hyssop branch and its flowers were chosen, because the children of Israel used as the purifying agent to escape God's wrath on the Egyptians; which can be found in **Exodus 12**. For instance, its carminative properties stimulate the downward passage of gas for safe expulsion from the body. Hyssop is an astringent, because it makes our muscles and limbs contract. Finally, the scarlet wool was used to symbolize the blood itself and it foreshadowed the robe put on Jesus before his crucifixion.

In passage nine, it explains that the priest and his assistants had to purify themselves after creating the agent for cleansing of sin. According to **Leviticus 16:26-28** they were unclean for ceremonies. They were unclean, because they came in contact with a dead animal and spiritually unclean, because of the debt of sin. Next, in passages nine through 13 we find that the ashes of the remains were gathered and stored in a clean place outside the camp. This mixture would be ready to mix with water for anyone that needed purification. Purification was necessary for anyone who touched a dead body and that person was unclean for seven days. you were also considered unclean if you entered the tent of another person who had died. Death was so pervasive that it corrupted open containers. contact with a corpse, human bones, contact with the secret Holy water, contact of anything to do with the graves, or touching the unclean person also brought impurity. **Haggai 2:13** This person required purification for themselves with Ash water. After the seven days waiting period they had to clean with Ash water on the third day and the seventh day. Finally, in **Leviticus 15:31** if an unclean person came in proximity of the tabernacle they were put to death.

17 through 22 it explains the mixing of the Ash from the red heifer, water in it a goat skin jar, and apply in the mixture with the hyssop branch on the third day and a seven day would make you clean. The Israelites made sure that they applied more to affected areas. of the skin. On the seventh day the unclean party sprinkle this mixture on himself and is his/her clothes. Then, they bathe themselves in flowing water. If you were a rebel, and did not follow this procedure, you qualified for death by rock or excommunicated from the community.

Skin	Red Hair	The Body	Ashes
Signified the dead of sin.	The Blood of Jesus.	Foreshowing Jesus's crucifixion.	The Sprinkling of Jesus's Blood to Forgive; Thus, making all making clean.

END TIME SIGNIFICANCE

The Dead Sea Scrolls were found in a cave. Scientists found a copper scroll which was in such poor condition that they had to tear it into strips. I love the imagery here! For example, the scrolls were torn into columns like we find scripture recorded in our Bible. Then, when Jesus was born He was covered in strips of rags. At His crucifixion, His clothing was torn into strips, but at his death Jesus was magnified and He showed us that sin was defeated and our way to enteral life was completed with the folded napkin. This is important, because even the rags point to the gospel of Jesus Christ. Finally, the scientist took several years to interpret the scroll. They announced it was like a treasure map, because directions were written to the ancient temple furnishings. The artifacts are important, because prophecy says that once the temple of Jerusalem is built and sacrifices are performed that Jesus will return to collect His saints. (**2 Thess, Matthew 24, and Rev. 11**)

In Jerusalem today, there are two groups focused on re-building the temple. The ash of the red heifer is important, because they must have pure ashes in order to be washed and sanctified. This is the first step in actually having service for the Jews. This service is known as the separation of water or the water of sanctification. This ceremony is performed before the Jews can enter their sanctuary. The men must dip in clean flowing water and get sprinkled with the ash. After, this process is complete they are considered sanctified and can enter the tabernacle. The Jews also use this ointment to separate the building and all its furnishings within for an offering to God.

Jesus is the picture of this sacrifice. This is the one of the only female offerings found in the Old Testament. Jesus (parallel to the red heifer) will return for His bride. His bride (saints) will be adorned with forgiveness. Christ at that moment will be our groom and He will connect himself to His bought -bride. So, what do you think is His wedding gift?

_____

_____

_____

How about the New Jerusalem brought down by heaven? (**2 Corn. 2:11**)

Hyssop

-Foreshadowed Jesus as a Holy Sacrifice.
- Is a disinfectant used to cleanse.
- It is also an antiseptic, sterile, and germ cleansing agent.
- Pushes gasses downward; which, has the result of passing gas.
- Its also an astringent; which, makes our muscles and limbs contract.

Cedar-Wood

- Prevents wounds from becoming septic.
- Cure for diarrhea, because it tightens the
muscles of the digestive system
- Destroys a cough by preventing phlegm. Phlegm is
what settles in the lungs that creates a block.

The S.O.A.P Method

A few years ago, Mom's Toolbox presented the SOAP technique for exploring God's Word. The S.O.A.P. system is a learning method that teaches us to stop and reflecting on God's conversation. It's simple tool! I use this method with my Sunday School class and in my private study also.

What does S.O.A.P. stand for?

_____

1. **Scripture** ~ Write the focal verse.
2. **Observation** ~ Write down two concepts of the passage. Record what you hear the Holy Spirit expresses to you.
3. **Application** ~ How does the communication pertain to your everyday life?
4. **Prayer** ~ Write a prayer established in the message.

Practice

Of course, we are going to use the above method in this section! Now, is a fine time to question, "What in the world, does soap, the SOAP method, and goats have to do with essential oil and our Bible study?" What do you get when you put the words goat, milk, and soap together? _____. That's so easy! – Goats' Milk Soap. Have you ever used it? _____ I and other historians, believe it's totally possible that God's Children knew how to combine oil, water, and milk to make soap. Great! Now that we have processed the why, lets assess some of the most familiar essential oils that would have used in the Old Testament time era. Below, you'll find a list of oils I've found. You may add to the list if you find one.

Lavender
Song of Solomon 4:13
Juniper
1 Kings 17:4-5
Job 30:4
Mint
Matthew 23:23
Luke 11:42
Rose
Isaiah 35:1
Cedarwood
Numbers 19:6
Cassia Exodus 30:24
Ezekiel 27:19

Those passages were very informative! Now, your study begins! Below you'll find a few S.O.A.P graphic organizers! Choose a few (three) essential oils that are your favorite and use the method. Then, make a note of how it felt completing the chart and if it was helpful.

S.O.A.P ONE

Scripture	Observation	Application	Your Prayer

S.O.A.P TWO

Scripture	Observation	Application	Your Prayer

I believe that one of the reasons God put me through college and gave me a teaching degree was to prepare me to write books. In these books, I believe that God wants we not only to reveal what He has given me, but also to teach you how to study His word. In my 38 years of life, I have been in several classrooms, and the methods I provide in my books come from those experiences. Most of the time I have to change them up a bit, because they are worldly, but with the Holy Spirit this is possible. I love how He links everything together. With the knowledge, He has given me I am able to infuse my love for crafts and creativity. For example, I'll provide you with my home-made goat soap recipe. Yes, you can make goat milk soap. I love to do this one with children! I do the steps one to eight at home and bring in a big slab of unscented soap. This process takes a fair amount of time.

But, by the time I teach them about how Jesus cleans us up inside and out I don't have the time to do all the steps. This recipe is also on YouTube under prebatching goat milk soap. Plus, it's in my book entitle, Remedies and Recipes Found in God's Backyard. If you just aren't a crafty person or don't have time to make a batch of your own- you can purchase my soap at **www. findinghealinginGodsbackyard.com.** Finally, I don't care if you buy it and say it's your creation. I'll give you permission to fib a bit!

Goat Milk Soap Recipe

Note: Watch my YouTube Channel for guidance!
https://youtu.be/WvAC6OSpDvs
(Romans 8: Cleaned through Jesus)

INGREDEINTS:

Goat's Milk 18oz	Distilled Water 1oz
Coconut Oil 20oz	Olive Oil 20oz
Rice Bran Oil 5oz	Avocado Oil 5oz
Castor Oil 4oz	Shea Butter 5oz
Sweet Almond Oil 5oz	Lye 9oz

All of these ingredients usually costs me 58.00$

STEP 1. My goats milk is frozen in 18 oz packs; so, the first thing to do is to crack the milk in small pieces. Then, use about 1oz of distilled water to help the milk dissolve.

STEP 2. Go ahead and set your crockpot to high. Grab a large bowl. Fill the sink ½ way with ice water. Use a bowl big enough to set-in your lye container.

STEP 3. Sprinkle about a 1/4 of your lye and start mixing. Make sure you mix slowly! Dumping causes clusters that are hard to dissolve. So, start with sprinkling about 1/4 of the lye and mix, mix, and mix again. After it melts you'll have goat's milk.

STEP 4. Once it melts a little, add another 1/4 of the lye and mix well. Repeat this process until you have used all of your lye. Your solution will look yellow after your lye is dissolved.

STEP 5. Place your bowl of lye and goats milk in a sink of cold water. Clean out your crockpot somewhat and add all your unmelted oils.

STEP 6. Melt the hard oils. This includes the coconut oil and the shea butter. 30 mint

STEP 7. Slowly, add the liquid oils to the melted oils, because this helps bring the temperature down.

STEP 8. Once we have the oils melted your Soap Making Process Begins and it's easy. You can add your essential oils to the melted oils in the kitchen sink. Hint: when adding your essential oils follow the recipes in this book. This will ensure your fragrance reaches the desired strength.

STEP 9. Take a stick blinder and mix the oils again. You can use a whisk, but that's a really long process. Add in the soap base in your sink.

STEP 10. Then slowly added mixtures together and blend well. For a more powerful smell add more essential oils. Some people like to add perfumed oils.

STEP 11 Pour the refined mixture into your molds. I use the smaller molds, because this protects my batch from overheating.

STEP 12. Next place your molds in the fridge or cellar to cool. Wait 24 hours before demolding. (Make sure your surface is level). Sometimes, the smells are not accurate, but within the next 24 hours a more appealing aroma will be delivered.

STEP 13. Cut your soap into the mold you want. Finally, wrap your soap in knitting not plastic, because the soap needs to breathe and add a label.

NOTE: To skip this long process visit www.findinghealinginGodsbackyard. com and purchase your all-natural soap!

For essential oil formals to create your Soap Zests please see <u>Essential Oil Recipes and Remedies found in God's Backyard:</u> The Purifying recipe is "by-far" my favorite blend! I love the aroma and I love the lesson! This recipe removes odors in the air, disinfects the environment, and it removes harmful micro-organisms from our skin, hair, air, and the digestive system. Every time, I use the purifying soap if reminds me of scripture. This is a great time to ask God to purify your inside as you are cleaning the outside. With children, we focus on topics of holiness, sin, the Spirit, mercy, repentance, relationships, sacrifice, and Baptism.

Lemon Soap
(Ease Dry-Skin)

Ingredients:

Melt and pour soap (we used goat's milk soap)
2 lemons, zested
2 tablespoons poppy-seeds
20 drops Lemon essential oil
Microwave safe glass bowl
Silicone mold
Rubbing alcohol in spray bottle (optional)

Directions:

1. Cut 1 pound of your soap base into small squares. (Most melt and pour soap bases come in 2-pound blocks. Just use 1/2 of the soap base now and save the rest for a different project.) One pound of soap can make between 4 and 8 bars of soap depending on the size of your mold.

2. Place cut-up soap into a microwave safe bowl. Place in microwave and melt for 30 second intervals, stirring in between. We recommend stirring with a popsicle stick for easy cleanup. Once soap is melted, set aside. If you don't want to use a microwave, you can also use a double boiler.

---

3. Zest 2 lemons and add zest to melted soap along with the poppy-seeds.
4. Add Lemon essential oil and stir until combined.
5. Pour soap into mold. Spray with rubbing alcohol for a smooth top free of bubbles.
6. Let soap harden for 2-3 hours. Once hard, it is ready to be used.

The Anointing Oil

Class Script

(YouTube video Available)

1. For methods of hospitably, sanitization, and fragrances. <u>Song of Solomon 1:3</u>
2. To bring physical healing of plagues, ailments, and disease. <u>Mark 6:13</u>
3. "high priests were anointed with oil" · <u>Matthew 6:17</u>
4. "he was anointed as the organizational candidate of the party" · <u>Luke 4:18</u>
5. Pouring essential oils over the heads of people to show
6. reverence and contentment. <u>Matthew 6:17</u>
7. Dipping or pouring essential oils on tangible items to set them apart as God's instruments <u>Ex. 40:9</u>
"bodies were anointed after death for burial" <u>Matthew 26:12</u>

In preparation of a bride in marriage. <u>Ruth 3:3</u>
To bring legal change through new agreements.
The disciples and Jesus casted out devils.
Metaphorically to represent the change in an unclean heart to purified heart.

Teaching Method:

Fold paper in half 3 times to get 8 squares. Students write one fact in each square.

What did people in Biblical times use Anointing oil?

_____

_____

_____

The word anoint appears more than 156 times in scripture. In ancient days, the anointing oil was prepared from oil alone and often with the addition of flowers, fragrant herbs, gums, resins, seeds, spices and other botanicals. We perceive in **Matthew 26:7** and **John 12:3-8** that the oils are known as precious ointment. The precious ointment existed as the costliest medicine to the ancient people. The <u>Precious oils</u> that transpired were myrrh, frankincense, and spikenard. Moreover, in **Mark 6:13** the ointment was used to drive away demons. In **John 9:11**, the scripture used mud of the ancient world to cure blindness. The power of prayer granted the healing. I can't find anyone that has rubbed mud on their eyes and now they can see. Jesus's could have healed him minus the mud, but the Jews (and us today) always needed a sign.

In history books, Jews did not just apply a couple of drops to someone's forehead. The biblical practice was to pour the oil on the head. The head was messaged. Prayers for the person was brought by the children of God in the form of petitions. The oil actually ran down the face and beard and onto the clothing. In those days, hygiene was lacking, and the oil would have provided a pleasant odor and a shield from germs.

How do you anoint someone?

_____

_____

_____

The power of anointment is not in just dropping a couple drops of oil onto someone's forehead as stated above. This action has a greater meaning in symbolism. God's medicine is not in just one oil or in one application. God's medicine came in various forms, because there are several different types of essential oils and several different illnesses to treat. For example, if I was being anointed for a backache, it would make more sense to, message five drops of peppermint, rosemary, and basil on the sore area; rather then, dropping a couple drops of plain olive oil onto my forehead. The combining of peppermint, rosemary, and basil creates God's medicine. When blended it produces a pain reliever, but prayer is needed to magnify God's medicine and produce healing.

Consider **Psalms 133:2!** This segment expresses that the odors of members aboding together in unity: "is like the precious ointment upon the head, that ran down the beard, even Aaron's beard: that went down his garments." An alternative to this passage and anointing oil is, in Ecclesiastes 9:8: "Let thy garments be always white; and let thy head lack no ointment." God's people poured it on! The precious oil was spread from head to toe.

The Bible reports an episode where the burning of incense immunized a plague. In the account of **Numbers 16:46-50**, Moses instructed Aaron to take a container of fiery coals and incense to the congregation. Aaron was to use this for an atonement for the people. Moses said act quickly, because a great plague from the Lord; has begun." Aaron followed Moses directions and the plague was not casted on his people. According to ancient recipes a variety of cinnamon was used. Today, we know cinnamon is antimicrobial, anti-infectious, and antibacterial. This means the formula would of broke down bacteria inside and outside. It would have killed the infection and stopped it from spreading. I would image scent of cinnamon and myrrh was sweet. The combination of the aroma would have made the camp more inviting. The smell of the camp would be similar to us entering a home that smelled great!

Where can anointing take place?

_____

_____

_____

Have you ever seen an anointing outside of the church house? If so when and where?

_____

_____

_____

The most common biblical act, modern Christians, associate with the word anoint is in the action of anointing. Many churches only refer to the term anoint in one scripture. This scripture comes from the book of James. James instructs the sick to call on the elders of the church, be anointed with oil, and ask God for the healing. However, it's interesting James did <u>not</u> say do this <u>only</u> in the <u>temple</u>, but the temple has become the place our society has determined to be where healings occur.

Teachers Note:

I challenge you, as you teach the lessons in this manual, that you also use God's blend to anoint, right in your class.

Where did Jesus perform His anointings (healings)?

Let's just consider a few healings in the following scriptures. Your job, is to locate, read, and record what the Holy Spirit revealed to you, in the boxes!

Roman Centurion for Paralyzed Servant, at Capernaum and the Canaanite woman   <u>Matthew 15:28,</u>   <u>Luke 7:2-10,</u>
Demoniac in Synagogue, at Capernaum   <u>Mark 1:23-28</u>   <u>Luke 4:31-37</u>

Luke 7:2-10 2 "There a centurion's servant, whom his master valued highly, was sick and about to die. 3The centurion heard of Jesus and sent some elders of the Jews to him, asking him to come and heal his servant....

Please read the rest of the scripture and then paraphrase it in the space provided.

_____

_____

_____

Jesus judges the thoughts of the centurion as an act of faith. In fact, "great faith," because he believed without seeing! The Centurion believed in Christ's supernatural ability. He does not expect anything visible. I can only find twice where Jesus says that a person has great faith. One instance is this Roman centurion and then a Canaanite woman. The Canaanite woman pleads her requests for Jesus to heal her daughter. You'll find this account in **Matthew 15:28**. These two miracles prove that our faith transcends where we are born, our race, our birth privileges and the oil we use. When we anoint we are admitting our weakness and need for Jesus. His faith shows his acceptance and respect of Christ as Savior and his submission to His will.

Mark 1:23-28 and **Luke 4:31** tells us that Nazareth was dangerous for Jesus; therefore, He moves to Capernaum. While Jesus is teaching in the church; a man is there, and within him is an unclean spirit. Jesus was new to Capernaum and His fame was not recognized. As He begins to preach, the unclean spirit becomes restless in the man. He is unable to control what comes out of his mouth. This unclean spirit wanted everyone to know who was speaking to them. Perhaps, to drive Jesus out or ruin his mission. Then, the unclean spirit wanted to discredit Jesus and began to lie. The word of Jesus touched the man and tossed the unclean spirit out of him. When we are anointed Jesus does just that for us. Sometimes, we have spirits of depression, anger, or sickness that we need Jesus to cast out. Just one word uttered from the lips of Jesus is all that was needed that day and all that is today.

Jesus performed his healings in the church, but He also touched people where ever He adventured. Today, Jesus can certainly touch you at an altar of prayer, but He can also touch you no matter where you travel. So, if Jesus can touch us where-ever we go; then, why do we only see anointings in the church house?

_____

_____

_____

Through my book signings and people allowing me to come teach I've been fortunate to witness anointings in different places. It was awkward at first, but after Jesus showed-up it was all worth it. I anoint according to the sickness. Below, I have provided a chart of examples. You may copy and use them for the glory of God!

<u>Gastroesophageal reflux disease</u> 1 drop Peppermint essential oil 1 teaspoon honey 1/2 teaspoon organic apple cider vinegar Glass of warm water
<u>Arthritis</u> frankincense, lemongrass, rosemary, and mix in coconut oil
<u>Bronchitis</u> Lavender, Peppermint and Frankincense are most commonly used to help lung congestion.
<u>Back Pain</u> Mix with chamomile oil, 5 drops of ginger oil, and 10 ml Jojoba Oil. Gently massage the oil blend on the back; preferably you can get a hot compress (Like my aroma-therapy flaxseed bags) on your back 15 minutes after the oil massage.
<u>Headache</u> Lavender, Marjoram, and Patchouli, and mix in vitamin E oil.
<u>Dry Scalp</u> tea tree oil for dandruff, rosemary to grow hair faster, lavender and peppermint for dry scalp and to stimulate hair growth.

The following chart includes some more common complaints and its Biblical Antidote.

Complaints	Essential Oils
Stress	Combine the oils with coconut oil and place on the back of the neck. Lavender, lemon, bergamot, peppermint, vetiver, pine, and ylang ylang

Insomnia	Combine the following oils Lavender, Chamomile, jasmine, benzoin, sandalwood oil and ylang ylang; with coconut or avocado oil. Place on bottoms of feet and on your forehead. Defuse or burn the oils in a defuser or candle.
Anxiety	Lavender, bergamot, rose, clary sage, lemon, Roman, chamomile, orange, sandalwood, geranium, and pine All of these oils are good! I create oil wax candles and goat milk soap.
Depressed Mood/ Sorrow	Grapefruit, wild orange, tangerine, lemon, and peppermint Mix these oils in your shampoo and anoint yourself while washing your hair.
Pain	Deep Blue, Peppermint, chamomile, lavender, and jasmine
Nausea and vomiting	Mint, ginger, lemon, orange, ginger, dill, fennel, chamomile, clary sage, and lavender Mix with coconut oil and apply to the tummy and belly button.
Tinnitus (Ringing in the Ear)	Aromatherapy experts say that essential oils such as cypress, lemon, **rosemary**, rose, chamomile and **lavender**, help to soothe the symptoms and anxieties created by tinnitus. The methods of utilizing essential oils for natural tinnitus relief include vaporization, massage, inhalation, compress and bathing.
High Blood Pressure	Mix several oils, such as rose, lemon, cinnamon, and cassia. Add them to a diffuser or candle. Oil vapor is diffused throughout the air and the scent is inhaled. This olfactory signal is received in the medulla where your blood pressure is controlled in the brain. The smooth muscles that make up the blood vessels relax; thus, lowering blood pressure

| Toenail Fungus | Tea Tree Oil, orange, and lavender. All are both antiseptic and fungicidal remedy. First clean areas on and around the infection with rubbing alcohol then apply undiluted tea tree oil directly to the affected nails and let it soak in. |
| Neuropathy | Eucalyptus, rosemary, and eucalyptus essential oils are also very helpful in improving diabetic neuropathy symptoms when combined with aloe Vera gel. |

FEET WASHING

CLASS SCRIPT

(YouTube Video Complete)

Because, I actually witnessed two wonderful women in ministry argue on the following topic this. This lesson was born. Their question, Did Jesus wear sandals? Yes, but they were not flip flops! Sandals in Greek was: Na'alayim. According to their history, sandals were made of leather. The sandal was created solely to protect the feet from the rugged terrain. (Genesis 14:23, Isaiah 5:27). No one, in this time era wore sandals in the house nor in the sanctuary. (Exodus 3:5 and Joshua 5:15). Only the poorest of people would walk the streets without sandals. (Deuteronomy 25:19) or of mourning (2Samuel 15:30 and Ezekiel 24:17,23). In addition, Jesus in fact wore sandals! Read the following text and record "why" in the space provided!

John 1:27

_____

_____

_____

The night before Jesus was taken He washed the feet of his disciples. The disciples were also questioning His actions. All the disciples knew that the ones who washed the feet of others were the lowest forms of servants. This was a position no one wanted in their society. Just as I would not like to have the occupation as a restroom attendant. Smells do not bother me. It's all the risks involved. Plus, I hate do any kind of scrubbing. The people in Jesus's day used all natural cleaners. It is a great idea for us to use the all natural cleaners to purify our environment.

What are some of the all-natural cleaners used during Jesus's day?

_____

_____

_____

What are some of the all-natural products we can use to purify our environment?

_____

_____

_____

The top five essential oils I use in my home are as follows: Lavender, Lemon, basil, thyme, peppermint, orange, and melaleuca. According to the research, God's people would have had access to lavender, basil, thyme, eucalyptus, peppermint, and melaleuca.

Lavender fights fungus. I used lavender to wipe off my kitchen countertops and basins. I also use lavender on my dyer balls that I place in the dyer as fabric softener.

Lemon, basil, and Thyme cuts through grease and grime. I regularly use lemon, basil, and thyme in my fish recipes, but I also use these oils to clean my silverware.

I use **peppermint** oil in a scrub to clean my cookware and sink.

Eucalyptus essential oil increases its power when combined with baking powder and I use this formula to clean my mattress. Eucalyptus is also a fragrant floor cleaner.

Orange is my favorite essential oil for cleaning. I use orange to shine my floor and in my furniture polish.

Melaleuca can be an antibacterial cleaner. We use melaleuca to clean surfaces to fight germs that causes the flu and other illnesses. Mixed with olive oil, we clean the door jams of the shower door and this fights mildew.

During Jesus's last dinner he asked the disciples (and us) to do two things. One was to take communion and one was to perform foot washings. Some ministers thank that the preacher should perform Jesus's request, but it's my opinion that all the church members should complete Jesus's request. The best time to have a foot washing service would be around our Passover or during Easter services.

Read **John 13:1-11** and determine for yourself if foot washing should be done and to whom should do it. In the space record your answer.

_____

_____

_____

Complete the chart below to help you answer:
The difference between Ought and Should.

Luke 18:1	
Acts 5:29	
Eph. 5:28	
1 John 4:11	
John 13:15	

(Note to for the teacher: Copy and cut out the following scripture. Before class, give them to good oral readers. Complete the above chart with the class)

Luke 18:1 ¹And he spake a parable unto them to this end, that men ought always to_pray, and not to faint;

John 13:15 ¹⁵For I have given you an example, that ye should <u>do</u> as I have done to you.

1. 1 John 4:11 ¹¹Beloved, if God so loved us, we ought also to <u>love</u> one another.

Acts 5:29 ²⁹Then Peter and the other apostles answered and said, We ought to <u>obey</u> God rather than men.

Ephesians 5:28 ²⁸So ought men to <u>love</u> their wives as their own bodies. He that loveth his wife loveth himself.

Note that in John 13:4 that Jesus took off his garment. In Jewish history that left only a small covering of his garment. This garment was only worn by the slave or the servant. What would this action have created in the minds of the disciples?

_____

_____

_____

This was a loving act of humility. This action represented Jesus laying aside his life for us. When we take part in a foot washing ceremony we are showing our ability to also lay aside our life, our time, and our desires. The action of kneeling in front of a brother or sister in Christ portrays our willingness to serve one another as Christ served us.

Locate the following verses in the scripture. These verses portray foot washing in a certain light. What does foot washing represent?

Genesis 18:4

_____

_____

_____

Genesis 24:32

_____

_____

_____

2 Samuel 11:8

_____

_____

_____

The next thing I would like to point out to you is in **verse 27.** Jesus even washed the feet of Judas. Jesus knew that Judas was a true enemy of Christ; however, Jesus still washed his feet. Notice that Judas had not committed the sin yet in time, but Jesus already knew it. So, was Judas an enemy of Christ in that moment?

_____

_____

_____

Rather we believe he was not yet an enemy or that Judas was an enemy is not my point. The point is Jesus our Redeemer stilled loved even Judas. How many times have we been the enemy? – But Jesus still loves us. What does this say to your heart?

_____

_____

_____

Should we also love the enemy? _____ Should we also humble ourselves? _____

In **John 13:13-14** Jesus himself explains why he washed their feet. We probably had an answer right up front. Why is that? This is because we have the Holy Spirit guiding our thoughts and understandings. Jesus calls us to freely serve Him, God, and mankind.

What does **1 John 3:17** ask us to do?

_____

_____

_____

Finally, why does Jesus call us to foot washing? **John 13:15**

_____

_____

_____

What is our reward? **John 13:17**

_____

_____

_____

In **John 13:1-3** Jesus washed the feet of his disciples after dinner; therefore, a foot washing church service should come after communion. I admit, during my bible study classes we often do not observe communion before foot washing. I do ask everyone to come with clean feet! The fact Jesus washed their feet after dinner eliminates the idea that Jesus washed dirty feet. In the Jewish society, the disciples would have washed their feet upon arrival. If you re-examine the following verses- note when they were expected to wash their feet.

Genesis 18:4

_____

_____

_____

Genesis 24:32

_____

_____

_____

2 Samuel 11:8

_____

_____

_____

Prayer Cloth

Class Script

(YouTube Video Available)

The Biblical basis for the prayer cloth actually began in the book of Matthew, we observe (**Matthew 9:20–22**) the story of a woman who had suffered severe bleeding for twelve years. She had spent all she had on prescriptions and physicians, but still was not healed. She undoubtedly heard about Jesus. She managed to touch the hem of Jesus' cloak, believing this simple contact would heal her. Jesus answered in verse 22, telling her, "Your faith has made you well." Also, in **Matthew 14:34–36,** the people of Gennesaret had a similar thought. Absolutely all the sick heard the fame of Jesus and desired to touch only the hem of Jesus' garment.

I would like for us to begin way back in the new testament in Isaiah. According to **Isaiah 10:27** (JUB) 27 And it shall come to pass in that day that his burden shall be taken away from off thy shoulder and his yoke from off thy neck, and the *yoke shall be consumed in the presence of the anointing.* Our problems and illnesses will be taken away by the anointing of God. The entire practice of the anointing cloth and creating a prayer cloth comes from **Acts 19:11–12.** 11 And God wrought special miracles by the hands of Paul: 12 So that from his body were brought unto the sick handkerchiefs or aprons, and the diseases departed from them, and the evil spirits went out of them. This conveys how handkerchiefs that Paul had merely touched were carried to the sick, in hopes that people would be healed of diseases and evil spirits. The word handkerchiefs according to the dictionary means: a square of cotton or other finely woven material, typically carried in one's pocket and intended for blowing or wiping one's nose. The Bible Dictionary States the following: "Only once in Authorized Version (**Acts 19:12**). The Greek word (sudarion) so rendered means properly "a sweat-cloth." It is rendered "napkin" in **John 11:44 ; John 20:7 ; Luke 19:20.**" Below, I have left you some space to investigate the scriptures more thoroughly!

John 11:44

_____

_____

_____

Teacher's Note:

John **11:44** is a very familiar scripture. There have been many lessons taught, sermons preached, and songs sang about the resurrection of Lazarus. In this study, I want to give you a little more depth in the account of Lazarus. In John, the grave mummification was the custom of Eastern countries including the Egyptians and Jews. Jesus's powerful words echo throughout the pages of scripture. In today's language, these words would sound something like this, "Untie his hands and feet. Let him plant his feet firmly on the ground. Then, let him go freely!" This is the true definition of anointing! The prayer cloth is one way to say, cast out the evilness with this woman, cast her sins as far as the east as to the west, and drive out the sickness from her body. Then, let her plant her feet firmly on the ground and go in freedom.

John 20:7

_____

_____

_____

Teacher's Note:

In this scripture, we find Peter and Mary outside the tomb of Jesus. We understand their account of Jesus's grave clothes! His wrappings were neatly stacked and stringently placed! Jesus was anointed before He ever became man, but here we notice that Jesus simply replaced his grave clothes with one that is enterally significant. Furthermore, Jesus's Earthly clothes were even anointed. On several accounts, many people believed that "only one touch" of his garment would heal them completely.

Luke 19:20

_____

_____

_____

Teacher's Note:

Luke is still describing clothing in this passage, but it has a more spiritual meaning. The rich man is unsaved, and the poor man is saved. The angles both have the same task. One is to render the saved to paradise and one is to render the soul in Hades. The clothed is the saved person and we simply lay down our clothing and positions on Earth and gain heaven. However, the unsaved must be snatched from their clothing, positions, and family. The saved are truly anointed and set free in Heaven, but the unsaved are naked in a spiritual sense and sent into uttermost destruction.

Was the clothing of Jesus ever ripped?

I have only seen one source that has informed me of the tearing of Jesus's garment, but most preachers will tell you that Jesus's clothes were never torn. I can find no evidence, in the Bible, that concluded Jesus' "(sudarion)" had ever been torn and people were healed. However, Jesus's clothes were torn during is inexcusable torture before his death. For example, 24. And they prayed, saying, "You, Lord, the Knower of the hearts of all, show which one of these two You have personally chosen . . ." 26. Then they cast their lots; and the lot fell on Matthias, and he was numbered with the eleven apostles (**Acts 1:24, 26**, HBFV throughout). Here are some citational passages for you to investigate:

Leviticus 16:8, Proverbs 16:33, 18:18, Acts 1:24 – 26

_____

_____

_____

What part of Paul's attire was used as the healing cloth?

Paul or God's people in scripture never called the handkerchief a "prayer cloth." The churches Paul wrote to had a custom that the men would wear a wrapped piece of cloth found on their heads. Theses skull caps serve a simple task. The sweat band simply caught their sweat. The New Testament Biblical leaders tore these long pieces of cloth to create handkerchiefs. The sweatband then was known as a handkerchief. Paul in Acts did in fact anoint this cloth and pray over it. When the sick received the cloth, the person was healed according to their faith.

Let's take a moment and examine the clothing Paul would have worn. (I usually use two teens for this section) The main pieces were a tunic, a loincloth, a waist belt, a money pouch, a cloak of robe, a ring, and the skull cap. In the chart, I have provided scriptures and important information. Please locate and read each scripture. (I would have assigned these scriptures before the lesson began).

Exodus 28:7 7It is to have two shoulder pieces attached to two of its corners, so it can be fastened.

Exodus 28:9-14 9 "Take two onyx stones and engrave on them the names of the sons of Israel 10in the order of their birth-six names on one stone and the remaining six on the other. 11Engrave the names of the sons of Israel on the two stones the way a gem cutter engraves a seal. Then mount the stones in gold filigree settings 12and fasten them on the shoulder pieces of the **ephod** as memorial stones for the sons of Israel. Aaron is to bear the names on his shoulders as a memorial before the LORD. 13Make gold filigree settings 14and **two braided chains of pure gold,** like a rope, and attach the chains to the settings.

John 19:38	
_____	
_____	

Numbers 15:37-38	Tassels on the corners Matthew 23:5 – Expensive silk wide sleeve and Blue Fringes
Tunic – An inner garment made from wool or cotton. Usually tucked under the belt. Exodus 28:40	
Loin cloth undergarment Exodus 28:42	
Waist Belt	
Money Pouch Mark 6:8	
Cloak or Robe Exodus 28:4	Royalty or Commoner
A ring	Often pushed in mug or wax for their signatures
Skull Caps/Turban Job 29:13-15	With bands of cloths around the edges
Exodus 39:29	Linen Girdle

Exodus 28:3-5 3Tell all the skilled workers to whom I have given wisdom in such matters that they are to make garments for Aaron, for his consecration, so he may serve me as priest. 4These are the garments they are to make: a breastpiece, an ephod, a robe, a woven tunic, a turban and a sash. They are to make these sacred garments for your brother Aaron and his sons, so they may serve me as priests. 5Have them use gold, and blue, purple and scarlet yarn, and fine linen.

Headwear (This is the section to have your teens model)

Depictions show some Hebrews and Syrians bareheaded or wearing merely a band to hold the hair together. Hebrew laborers certainly also dressed in head coverings. Their coverings were comparable to the modern keffiyeh. They made their keffiyeh from a generous square piece of knitted cloth. They would fold the fabric diagonally in half to create a fairly large triangle. The fold was worn across the forehead. The keffiyeh insecurely covered their back and shoulders. This was held tight with a long piece of fabric known as the sweatband. Wealthy men and women wore a something that resembled a turban. This was usually woven into a hat and it was shaped varied greatly.

The first modern use of a prayer cloth may have been by the Mormons. Then, as the practice faded in Mormonism, it grew in the Pentecostal church. Today, the tradition may be found in the Roman Catholic Church and throughout Christian Churches across the United States. Currently, the prayer cloth is not anointed with sweat from those who pray over it, but rather it's anointed with a fatty oil like vegetable. As more Christians learn how to use essential oils for healing we will see more churches using oils with a mood stabilizer. Churches could use vegetable oil, but also include citrus or peppermint to boost happy feelings.

Most Christians that believe in the prayer cloth have an idea on its meaning. What's yours?

_____

_____

_____

Most Christians believe the prayer cloth is merely a reminder that a group of people are praying for a friend or family member in need. A church usually adheres to the following scriptures in James. **James 5:14** Is anyone among you sick? Let them call the elders of the church to pray over them and anoint them with oil in the name of the LORD. The elders of the church then anoint the cloth with oil and pray for whatever need pertains. Some only believe it should be men and have actually kicked out the women! But, I believe a young man or woman could be an elder. An elder means who have grown up spiritually. For this reason, I believe the square should be larger than a one by one square of fabric. This anointed cloth should also serve as a reminder to pray.

More disconcerting, is the belief that the oil or sweat the prayer cloth is anointed with acts as a point of transfer. People believe the blessings of God are given to the recipients. This idea surly comes from the Holy Anointing Oil of Moses, because God told him to anoint certain things in the temple. This anointing was for meaning reasons. However, if you anoint a piece of cloth say with clove, cinnamon, eucalyptus and rosemary, you'll have an excellent cleaning rag. The chemical properties in clove, cinnamon, eucalyptus, and rosemary are all antibacterial; therefore, you have an all-natural and non-toxic cleaner. When the oils are placed in a soy wax candle or diffuser in the air it can be very stimulating and heartening. On the other hand, some people believe that the power of God is on the cloth and that power casts out demons. I agree, because my prayers are heard and answered always by God? Aren't yours? Scripture tells us that one job of Jesus is to set at the right hand of Father to hear our prayers. Finally, just the mention of the name of Jesus all evil disperses. Therefore, people in the hospitals often put the cloth on the area that needs a touch from God and are healed.

Perhaps, the most disturbing craze, especially on the web, is the use of prayer cloths as a fund-raising device. Prosperity gospel televangelists will pray over it for a fee. Then, the bigger the donation, the better the chance of healing you receive. So, are the televangelists on the same level as Apostle Paul? Brothers and sisters, I think you should be in a church, because God ordained this not for Him, but for us. It's in church these things are discussed, and this could help you from being deceived. 2 Peter 2:2-3 warns believers that others will take advantage of their faith. Then, 1 Corinthians 9:14 Paul tells us that gifts from God cannot be bought or sold. I think you should follow the scripture of James and Paul and stay with the word. Do not deceive and may you not be deceived!

CLASS 10

ANOINTING THE FEET

CLASS SCRIPT

What are the missing parts?

In this lesson you'll learn the benefits of feet washing, the steps in the process, what ingredients to use, and the mystery Jesus wanted to reveal.

Read John 13:3-18 allowed! (When I first began to teach; I actually highlighted the verses I'm going to point out in the lesson) (I also do this lesson as part of a foot-washing ceremony.)

One is as follows:

John 13:3-18 3 Jesus knew that the Father had put all things under his power, and that he had come from God and was returning to God; 4so he got up from the meal, took off his outer clothing, and wrapped a towel around his waist. 5After that, he poured water into a basin and began to wash his disciples' feet, drying them with the towel that was wrapped around him. 6He came to Simon Peter, who said to him, "LORD, are you going to wash my feet?" 7Jesus replied, "You do not realize now what I am doing, but later you will understand." 8 "No," said Peter, "you shall never wash my feet." Jesus answered, "Unless I wash you, you have no part with me." 9 "Then, LORD," Simon Peter replied, "not just my feet but my hands and my head as well!" 10Jesus answered, "Those who have had a bath need only to wash their feet; their whole body is clean. And you are clean, though not every one of you." 11For he knew who was going to betray him, and that was why he said not every one was clean. 12When he had finished washing their feet, he put on his clothes and returned to his place. "Do you understand what I have done for you?" he asked them. 13 "You call me 'Teacher' and 'LORD,' and rightly so, for that is what I am. 14Now that I, your LORD and Teacher, have washed your feet, you also should wash one another's feet. 15I have set you an example that you should do as I have done for you. 16Very truly I tell you, no servant is greater than his master, nor is a messenger greater than the one who sent him. 17Now that you know these things, you will be blessed if you do them. 18" I am not referring to all of you; I know those I have chosen. But this is to fulfill this passage of Scripture: 'He who shared my bread has turned against me.'

According to Jesus, in verse three, there was something only Jesus knew. The disciples did not know, and no other man knew. What was this fact?

_____

_____

_____

Do you understand the mystery?

_____

_____

_____

There is the part that the disciples didn't understand. The disciples did not understand the <u>transfer of power</u>. When we anoint the feet of brother, sister, family, or friend we perform an action Jesus required. The Scripture States, If I wash you not; you are not part of me. So, Paul volunteers Jesus to anoint every part of his body. Jesus even asked do you know why have I done this to you? And the answer is because he loves us, because he serves us, and because he has humility. When we wash one another's feet, because love is an action. This is one way to demonstrate our willingness, to come down as low as a servant, and serve one another. Kneeling below physical also informs us that we are all on the same level. Not one that one person is smarter or better than the other person. Finally, we wash one another's feet in accordance to God's word.

We are supposed to wash one another's feet for all these reasons, but let's continue to dig a little dipper so we can understand the mystery. We preform feet washing to receive God's blessing. We wash one another's feet and even our own to show that we believe, obey, and we have faith. The application part is us showing action. Today, we will take action.

When Jesus washed their feet, there was a spiritual transference.

This transference manifests us into a supernatural power. Wherever your feet go you shall possess and have dominion over the territory. Dominion over wicked spirits in darkness of places. By anointing your feet you'll have the supernatural victory. You won't go to the places where Christians should not be found. If you have fear your faith can remove any fears you have inside. Some people have a fear of driving or going to new places and the anointing of the feet they have power over it. Finally, we will have unspeakable joy, because we are being obedient. There is a secret high-five our spirit receives from Christ.

Have you ever felt and received this spiritual half of from God?

_____

_____

_____

The passage in **John 13:17,** States that, happy are you if you know and do these things. Whenever we put The Word of God into action the conditions change, but we must do all the spiritual protocols exactly as God says. There is a blessing! If we will follow God's instruction a reward for our obedience is granted. So, let's release our faith.

Let's apply what we learn from the word. It's simple!

As you pour your water and gather your supplies begin your conversation with Christ. Claimed the scripture but based on your own understanding. Declare and proclaim the part of Christ you need. Use the word "I". Again, using the word "I" tell Christ you were willing to Val down and become a faithful servant. Proclaim your faith, that Christ will impute whatever you need in order to for fill your calling.

Below is the prayer script I try to follow:

In the name of the mighty Jesus I dip my feet into this water. That part in which you spoke of in your word I proclaim it now. It is mine! In the holy name of Jesus. I speak to my heart tell my feet wherever you go you will proclaim the Lord Jesus. I do this in accordance to the word.

Feet, when you are called to stand, you will stand, and you shall not run. You shall not be moved. when you are to speak, you shall speak. Speak boldly and you will not be ashamed. Today, I hear the word of the Lord. You are empowered for greatness wherever you to tread you have power over it no powers of darkness shall overtake you. In the name of the mighty Lord Jesus you are protected. Now, go take the land for Jesus. Stand in boldness. Stand in liberty. Stand in freedom. God has given you it all. Jesus said God gave him all things; therefore, whatever she is lacking give it to her now Lord.

You are now ordained of God; therefore, you will not go to places you shouldn›t go to. Do not go Where the enemy may overtake you. You shall rise up and walk in what God has ordained. Walk in the ways of the Lord. Walk with the power of the Lord. Thank you, Lord Jesus, for transferring power and for transferring authority. Lord we now receive it, we now believe it, and it is ours. Amen!

If you have performed this in faith and you believe it. I know transference has occurred. Walk upright and may peace be with you.

WHAT IS A MANTLE IN SCRIPTURE?

A mantle can be a square piece of fabric, an apron, or the scarf on my head. Really it can be any fabric that comes in contact with a Christian. We contain the Holy Spirit which manifests itself. God is always flowing out of us.

Let's begin our study in:

2 Kings 2:1, 2Kings 2: 8- 15

In second Kings, Elijah is anointing Elisha, and they are asking for a double portion. When Elijah came into Elisha's field he put his mantle on Elisha. This meant he was transferring what Jesus gave him onto Elisha. The mantle was his anointed cloak.

After Elijah was called up into heaven Elisha preformed the parting of the sea. Then he walked on dry land on the other side. From this we can infer that God can manifest himself through People.

In **Luke 8:43-48 and Mark 5:25**, this is When Jesus walked the earth and virtue flowed out of him. Even throughout his clothing. Remember the lady with the issue of blood Jesus stopped the crowd and asked who touched me. Then told the crowd that He felt virtue come out of him.

We learn hear that God can flow through any vessel. This lady didn't have to touch the skin she just had to touch his garment and a virtue, or the power flew out of Him. She knew that power was in this man and anything he touched was powerful. According to her face she was healed.

Let's read Psalm 133:1-2!

We see the anointing upon Aaron did not stop on his four head, but it ran from the crown of his head down his face his beard and to his feet. This is why annoying teen is important. This is why God had his own special blend. To transfer his anointment one too he has people. In the scripture we see that he manifested himself through Aaron.

Find Psalm 45:6–8 and read it.

Again, we see here an anointing. Aloes and myrrh passed power through the garments of Aron. This action actually made Aaron glad. The oil from heaven anoints us with joy and happiness. It takes away all of our burdens and flows through our bodies and even exits onto our garments. then, by the virtue of your faith you can be made whole, happy, and with no sickness.

In **Acts 19:11–12** Paul said God brought wrath by his hands through his mantle's. First 12 so this is what Paul's handkerchiefs and aprons were passed to six people make them whole.

Let's read Matthew **14:35–36** as Jesus passed the crowd the only thing that people had to do was touch his clothing and they were made whole and healed. The power of God flows through our veins in the form of blood this is why we can claim healing. we can claim healing through his blood, because where Jesus is nothing that is impure, deceitful, or evil can remain. As long as you have faith in Jesus Christ and you can be well and you can be healed.

If you look at the scarf that I have on my head. I took it to a woman of God that believes in this transference and my scarf was anointed. This commandment scripturally allows me to be a teacher. Remember, it's not about the servant of God who anoints the cloths, it's about God that allows His power and virtue onto the material. This is why A faithful prayer in the book of James causes people to be healed. Therefore, during a circle prayer on anointing is more powerful then praying alone. Why? Because the saints of God allowed them to be vassals God could bless healing through.

THE CITY OF JERICHO

If you were alive in Jesus's day where would you purchase your essential oils?

_____

_____

_____

In verse one of **Luke 19:1-10** what city is noted?

_____

_____

_____

Zacchaeus lived just outside of the city of Jericho. The city of Jericho was known for its perfume. Jericho was thought to be a town with a nice aroma. I can envision Jericho has been similar to a large botanical garden or even the smell of my local flower shop. On the other hand, Jericho always suffers from a very hot climate; which would have increase the aroma of the oil. In addition, if you happen to be a skilled perfumer by trade; this, possibly would have your place of dwelling.

The city of Jericho was also the main route. The trail from Jericho to Jerusalem is 14 miles. Today, Jericho is controlled by Palestinians. It's also located north of the Dead Sea where the Jordan River Ends. Jericho is marked in scripture as the place where Joshua lead the battle of Jericho; which, is a prophetic picture of Christ's return. In addition, Jesus also healed the blind man and if you want the scoop, investigate the occurrence of the blind man being healed in **Luke 18: 35-43** for yourself! Moreover, Gilgal is located in Jericho towards the east. It's also known to be full of fresh water springs, but then just a few more miles you'll reach the banks of the Dead Sea.

In **Joshua 4:19** we find that the Israelites in Gilgal. What does scripture record?

_____

_____

_____

This scripture proves that Gilgal was full of water! People of the past and even today live near the water trough!

Finally, there are several scriptures that name Jericho as being the land of palm trees.

For example, locate the following scriptures:

Deuteronomy 34:3
Judges 1:16,
Judges 3:13
Judges 4:5.

What does **Luke 19:2** inform us about Zacchaeus?

_____

_____

_____

He was the cleverest tax collector. He was recognized for cheating his neighborhood and lining his pockets with their money.

How do you view a person that steals from his own people?

_____

_____

_____

Today, people that rob banks and the government are left alone, but people that steal from their neighbors are especially despised. He was a government official, but he was getting richer and he didn't care what he had to do to achieve his goal. He undoubtedly, had a very nice house with possessions of great value. What does scripture declare to us about owning essential oils.

In the space below record what **Proverbs 243-7** articulate.

_____

_____

_____

In fact, he probably bought, sold, and traded essential oils.

After investigating the Bible about Jericho, we realize that Jericho was a high traffic area. The people that resided there benefitted from assemblies of people. The citizens of this town routinely witnessed bands of travelers through their city. In fact, if you can visualize a parade, you would have an accurate picture of what the natives witnessed on Jesus's visit. In fact, this was their job. I'm sure the government of the city positioned children outside of the city to signal when travelers were on the route. Can you imagine the excitement of the people?

_____

_____

_____

I can, these towns people were not rich and sometimes were the poorest of the poor. I imagine the scene as being much like the flea market. When Jesus, His disciples and followers started on that route to Jericho I believe everyone in the city of Jericho was standing on the streets. Sure, all the merchants, traders, the afflicted, and the family of the affected where were there. Mothers brought their children and offered them to Jesus. Today, this scene would compare to a parade for our president. Mothers would offer their children to the president to get a picture or a kiss. The towns people of Jericho already knew that Jesus allowed the children to come to me. They also knew first-hand that one touch from Jesus improved that person's life. In addition, all the shopkeepers would have been ready. They would've been wheeling and dealing. Marketing and battering various items that would have sustained their life. In hopes of gaining revenue lodging food would be offer more than once. In my mental picture I visualized the perfumers trying to persuade customers giving out samples of their essential oils and perfume, musicians what have been playing harps, trumpets, and flutes.

What does Luke record in "The Word" in chapter 11 verse 4?

_____

_____

_____

Zacchaeus traveled all around collecting taxes and his money; therefore, he knew the road and perhaps every tree and plant on the route. He was also a great businessman. He knew how to plan out things and he had no problem following through or he would not have been a major player in business. I wonder, if the night before he planned out what he needed to make his plan successful? Did he create a map? I bet, he had his cloak and victuals satirically positioned at the door. He probably planned out what sycamore tree he was going to climb.

Why did Zacchaeus want to meet Jesus Perhaps, he learned of Jesus is power and miracles? Nevertheless, Jesus would've been a connection both for religious and political business. Therefore, in his line of business he had something to gain from meeting with Jesus. On the other hand, perhaps he was just curious about what Jesus look like. Maybe, Zacchaeus had heard that Jesus was the friend of sinners and Zacchaeus felt lonely; so, he wanted to friend. Regardless of his motives he sought to meet this man called Jesus.

Then, Scripture tells us that he ran ahead of the crowd. Found a sycamore tree and climbed it. I wish scripture would've given a picture of the tree we're just discussing the dimensions and how far he had climbed. In addition, according to travel agents, this sycamore tree is a travel destination in Jericho! So, do you think it's possible for the Jews to know the exact tree? Why or Why not?

_____

_____

_____

In the next verse, we find that scripture reports that Jesus stops? What happened next?

_____

_____

_____

Of course, if Jesus stopped; then, His enormous brigade coming out of Jericho also ceased at the base of the sycamore tree. I've never been to a parade where precession stopped in front of me. Then, call out my name and invite me to a divine appointment. This is exactly what happened to him. Afterwards, Jesus looked up and called for him to climb down the sycamore tree and Zacchaeus immediately climbed down the tree.

What do you envision this scene to portray?

_____

_____

_____

Jesus also yelled, "come down here; I'm going to stay with you tonight". I can't imagine how Zacchaeus felt at this moment, but the Bible records it was a happy unification! Additionally, in my curiosity, I question what other occurrences is keep secret in scripture. For example, what did Jesus his company discuss at the home of Zacchaeus? What was the conversational focused? How far did they have to travel to Zacchaeus house? Scripture only divulges that salvation was created in Zacchaeus's residential home. I believe to express his gratefulness Zacchaeus restores his debts to others. (**Matthew 6:9**) Finally, Zacchaeus can demonstrate his new life, his innovative way of thinking, and his new-fangled way of being a re-born person. How about you today? Do you crave what Zacchaeus was given? Do you need an encounter with Jesus.? The good news is that you also have a divine appointment. Are you eager to meet Jesus at your appointment this hour question? Undoubtedly? Jesus is waiting!

MATTHEW 26

The Anointing of Jesus.

First, read in **Matt 26:1-13** in its entirety.

Who anointed Jesus? Where was Jesus anointed?

_____

_____

_____

This event occurred in a town named Bethany. Bethany was a small village close to Jerusalem. The anointing occurred during dinner and it was in the residence of Simon the leper. Jesus healed Simon of his leprosy and, because of his healing he would have been the most grateful to Jesus. (^Luke 7:47: Therefore, I tell you, her many sins have been forgiven—as her great love has shown. But whoever has been forgiven little loves little.") His gratitude explains why he would have served Jesus in his dwelling. What a remarkable God we serve. One that continues with us till the end. One that would come to eat at someone's house that was sick. He was not afraid of the germs, he didn't have to use essential oils to purify the air, Jesus brought purification with him.

On a side note, if a woman anointed Jesus, then why can't a woman anoint the sick in the church?

_____

I actually went to a church that made the women sit down when they tried to follow the scripture of James. I was offended to the core. To my knowledge they still only allow the men to come up front when someone needs anointing. The scripture in James said call all the elders of the church not just the men. Some men were babes in Christ and did not know what was going on. I love when the Holy Spirit reveals the truth to me. Jesus came to set men and women free!

We don't know when exactly this occurred or what day of the week. For the purpose of this lesson we are concerned about Jesus's actual anointing. Looking back in Retrospect, in book one and two, the Feast of Passover, (**Exodus 12**) we learned that this feast is to celebrate God's removal of His children out of Egypt. The next feast is called the Feast of Unleavened Bread. God instructed His people to keep these feasts forever. The Feast of Unleavened Bread was to teach what bondage feels like. This feast took place a day or two after Passover. For example, the people had to clean their houses from top to bottom. We can relate. This is what we need to remember when we are Spring Cleaning. They cleaned their houses to get rid of even the breadcrumbs, because scripture says if leaven is found in your home then you are no longer part of the group. This says to us that God does not tolerate sin. Leaven is an example of sin.

In this scripture, I want to point out the words, "Son of Man" What does that mean?

_____

_____

_____

I was always taught this was a reference to mankind, but that is half of the truth. If you read the book of Ezekiel God always calls him son of man. So, we see this phrase means man. Please read **Daniel 7:13**, because this implies that Jesus is both man and God.

Scholars believe that John's sister Mary is doing the anointing, because he rises to his feet when she is done pouring. Myrrh came from Egypt. Egypt had a town called Alabaster. Therefore, the packaging for the essential oil of Myrrh was named, Alabaster. On page 89, of book one, you'll find an accurate photo of tree Myrrh. The essential oil of myrrh is said to smell like a grove of trees. Therefore, a great perfume or cologne can be created. For example, if I was making a perfume I would combine myrrh, distilled water, and tangerine. (Note: in class I have both combinations) If I was creating a cologne for men, I use myrrh, distilled water, and cedarwood in a glass spray bottle. When, John stood to his feet he yells out that was a pound! A

Roman pound would be 12 fluid ounces. (Note: for class I bring a can of soda for comparison.) In addition, myrrh was carried by men into battle. One specific battle that horrible, is described in **2 Cornicles 12:4-8**. The kingdom of Judah loses their battle with Egypt. Myrrh is the best essential oil for any open wounds; therefore, the men of Judah would have used this oil to combat gangrene.

The second oil of choice would have been the essential oil of spikenard. Spikenard, in biblical times was known as fragrant ointment. Also, a perfume and it strongly smells like a grove of trees. It is described as a Himalayan aromatic plant (Nardostachys jatamansi). In North American it is a perennial herb scientifically called, Aralia racemosa. A perennial herb lasts for a long time. It endures all seasons and continually be found in the Spring. The most related herb to us would be ginseng. Spikenard Oil is used a sedative and an herbal medicine to fight insomnia, birth difficulties, and other minor ailments. When combined with carrier oil as jojoba, sweet almond, or avocado, Spikenard Essential Oil can be applied to the skin or added to baths. Spikenard makes your skin shine. I add it to my homemade goat's milk lotions and soap. As a perfume I blend the essential oils of frankincense, lavender, myrrh, orange, and rose to create perfumes and colognes. I also ingest one drop to aide me constipation.

Present the unleavened bread:

Present the unleavened bread in two stacks of twelve, because God wanted this to be the show-bread in the temple. The show bread was the picture of God's son in the place where He works. The beginning of a new year for the Jews began in March. The fourteenth night was the Passover Feast. The fifteenth night marked the beginning of the Unleavened Bread Feast. The Unleavened Feast lasted seven days. This feast marked the removal of two million people leaving Egypt without time for their bread to rise. This feast reminds us all that The Blood of The Lamb delivers us from slavery.

Locate, read, and summarize the following two scriptures:

Leviticus 23:6

_____

_____

_____

Deuteronomy 16:3-5

_____

_____

_____

Today, the bread represents the body of Christ. We usually, partake of the body of Christ around Easter. Easter has replaced the feast of Passover and the feast of Unleavened Bread. Just to give you something to mediate on read the following example.

During the time Jesus walked the Earth Jews used stoning as their capital punishment. It was the Romans who enjoyed torturing people! The Romans lined the city streets with crosses. According to one historical paper I read it reported that sometimes the Romans ran out of trees. This horrific image entered my mind on my last Passover (which would have been our Easter). I was driving down the road and alongside the interstate was telephone pole after telephone pole. I was meditating on scriptures for this book and I begin to cry and thank Jesus for being my sacrifice. Can you imagine walking the streets of Jerusalem and above you were men who were still alive handing on crosses. I believe that our Godly compassion would cause this scene to be inconceivable. Both forms of punishment were inhuman, but if I had to choose, I would choose death by stoning, because at least this would be somewhat quicker. The Roman cross even makes beheadings and hangings seem like child's play. – With this information I challenge you to spend some time thanking Jesus for all He has given you!

Unleavened Bread

READY IN: 30 mins   SERVES: 16

INGREDIENTS NUTRITION

- 4 cups whole wheat flour
- 1 cup white flour
- 2 cups water
- 1/4 cup honey
- 1 1/2 teaspoons salt
- 1/4 cup oil

DIRECTIONS

1. Roll out to 1/8 inch thick.
2. Place on greased cookie sheet.
3. Score into about 1 inch squares.
4. Cut into 4 x 5 rectangles.
5. Bake at 400 degrees about 15 minutes.
6. In the first minutes of baking, prick bubbles that may form.

The Anointing of Jesus according to Mark

(Teacher and Students note: This lesson is a more indebt study of lesson six in book one.)

This biblical truth, takes place in the town of Bethany. According to Scripture, we are having a Passover dinner party. We are celebrating the fact that God took his children out of the slavery in Egypt! We are also celebrating that God sent a plague that killed all the firstborn children and first born of the livestock. We are remembering that in Egypt, God's death Angel passed over us. In the book of Hebrews, the angle was named The Destroyer.

Background Information about Passover:

— In Egypt, the children of God were instructed to put the blood of a lamb upon the doorpost and the lentil. I believe that they were excited about leaving Egypt, so; they went out and search for the perfect lamb. Remember, they had to have one with no spots, no blemishes, and no injuries.

— Then, when Jesus walked the earth the Sadducees and Pharisees could not even found find a fault within Jesus. Jesus was the best pearl heaven had to offer and he had no spots and no blemishes.

— The blood on the door covered the headboard and the side board, relates to today, because when we are surrounded by trouble, trials and even death, we need to be covered by the blood of the lamb.

— Some people worship all kinds of things in this world, but when they get ready to die they need the blood of the lamb. We will all gain the entrance to heaven only if we are covered by the Lamb of God. If you're not covered by the Lamb of God the red flames of hell will be our home for eternity.

The Characters that are involved are some very thankful people. We see Mary sister of Martha, Lazarus, Simon the leper, perhaps his family, the 12 disciples, and Jesus. I also believe that there may have been people who wanted to see the new clean Simon and the man who walked out of the grave. I can't imagine that emotions at this party! I've never witnessed this level of admiration and worship.

How would you describe the atmosphere?

_____

_____

_____

How would you decorate for your dinner party?

_____

_____

_____

What types of food would be involved?

_____

_____

_____

What two food related items does the scripture point out?

_____

_____

_____

Who is seated by the disciples?
Is Jesus at the end of the table?

_____

_____

_____

In Jesus's time and currently, in the Middle East, parties that sit down and eat together are known to mean more just friendly. For example, if you look at pictures of our government officials, you'll notice that they never are eating together. In the middle east, eating together is very significant. You'll never find a Middle Easterner eating with an enemy. Let's, throw in the word "known enemy," because Judas was an enemy of Jesus. In addition, when Middle Easterners do business they conduct business within their close ties first!

Meals involving Middle Easterners always include bread and salt. Notice, in Scripture, there are a few major references to the word salt. Salt, in the Middle East, has a significant meaning. For example, **Leviticus 2:13** 'And every offering of your grain offering you shall season with salt; you shall not allow the salt of the covenant of your God to be lacking from your grain offering. With all your offerings you shall offer salt.'[NKJV] Notice here, that the offerings were to be seasoned with salt, which is identified as the salt of the covenant.

Numbers 18:19 "All the heave offerings of the holy things, which the children of Israel offer to the LORD, I have given to you and your sons and daughters with you as an ordinance forever; it is a covenant of salt forever before the LORD with you and your descendants with you."[NKJV] (Aron's priesthood)

2 Chronicles 13:5 "Should you not know that the LORD God of Israel gave the dominion over Israel to David forever, to him and his sons, by a covenant of salt?" There is a Biblical phrase, for a two-way agreement, the inviolability of which was symbolized by salt. A Middle Eastern saying, "There is bread and salt between us," meant that a relationship had been confirmed by sharing a meal. Salt symbolized the life and enduring nature of the alliance. In the Old Testament, salt appears in the relationship between God and Israel (**Leviticus 2:13**). As a purifying agent and preservative in the sin offering, salt symbolized the indissoluble nature of the covenant between God and Israel. [Elwell, W. A., & Beitzel, B. J. (1988). In Baker encyclopedia of the Bible (p. 538). Grand Rapids, MI: Baker Book House.] For more information on the deeper meaning of salt in scripture refer to chapter eight.

Let's get back to our text! Please, read **Mark 14:1-21 and Mark 14:25-26!**

Why would they have anointed Jesus with spikenard?

_____

_____

_____

In the following three paragraphs we will do some studying on this topic. Please number the uses of Spikenard from 1 to 20. Then, complete the chart! Uses of Spikenard....

1.	11.
2.	12.
3.	13.
4.	14.
5.	15.
6.	16.
7.	17.
8.	18.
9.	19.
10.	20.

Let's focus on the effects of Spikenard on the body. (Please watch the video on YouTube for a visual example.) Spikenard poured directly onto His scalp and hair would have killed or repealed any issues of lice, parasites, and bugs. This would've also stopped any type of scalp itch. It would've gave his hair a glow. In addition, the scent of spikenard would have been soothing to the skin. Spikenard would also have prompted hair growth and reduced the chance of graying hair. Jesus would have been lavished with the scent, because it is a great man's cologne. Let's move our focus, on down to the face, and to the beard of Jesus. Spikenard has awesome effects on our wrinkles. Yet, it enhances his countenance. It provides a healthy glow. Therefore, when Jesus's face and beard was saturated with oil His skin illuminated. I'm sure his countenance was different from a regular person, but I'd imagine the spikenard would just magnify that glow. On the other hand, I do not like to imagine that our precious Savior had any type of scrapes, bruises, or even acne, but spikenard is a very good treatment for all skin blemishes. For example, if you had a mole and you constantly used spikenard, we would see the mole actually diminished in size, shape, and color.

Now, move down your focus to the neck! Everyone knows this is the home of the throat and thyroid. If Jesus's throat was hurting due to all of his lectures spikenard would seep into the skin, to help clear any infections. Again, let's move down to the abdomen. Spikenard is a very good Essential Oil that decreases gas and constipation discomfort. For example, by rubbing your abdomen with spikenard it helps your food digest and empty toxins. If you are pregnant, stay away from spikenard, because it stimulates the uterus. Now, if your babies due date has past, using spikenard, in this area, may help you go into labor. Finally, allow your focus to concentrate on your eyes. If you have trouble with your eyes rub spikenard on your toes, because you can't put spikenard into your eyes. To help digest and sleep rub two drops into the skin on the top of your feet.

Overall, one of the most important reasons why Mary would have used spikenard is that it affects the nerves in the brain. Meaning, that it would provide not only Jesus, but his disciples and everyone in the room with mental clarity! Which, they all would've needed in order to understand Jesus's death, burial, resurrection, and Holy Communion. Spikenard achieves these effects simply! For example, when the aroma is breathed into the nostrils, the nerves locate the aroma, and it automatically makes the body calm down. Which, makes the actions of Judas Iscariot ironic! Judas was God's treasurer! He kept track of all the donations and money the twelve disciples held. However, he was one of the biggest thieves of his time. Judas was not concerned with the poor. He was upset, because he could have controlled how much money they would have received from selling the essential oil. He would have been able to still a significant amount from that transaction.

Next, we see Judas orchestrating the trade of Jesus for a slave wage. Do you think this was the last straw for Judas? Why or why not?

_____

_____

_____

Judas was not concerned with the poor at all. He was concerned with himself getting richer. Many people today have this mentality. Have you ever been part of a "soul winning group"? Does the following comment sound familiar? -Why, are you worried about my soul when you should be feeding the poor or opening a soup kitchen? Many churches are worried about how much good they can be seen doing rather than treating the cause of the issue. There is a domination worried about socializing church. Jesus in our scripture told us that we will always have the poor, but that the Earth would only have Him for a little longer. The Bible instructs us to help the poor and we will be repaid in heaven. However, our first job is to spread the gospel and He would give the increase. Then, we are supposed to teach them all about the Bible. Some people are still deflecting their purpose to prosper their own pockets. Some, people argue that Judas Iscariot's role has been taken over by our government. Our government robs the poor and gives to the rich. Our money is drafted from our paychecks and then we have no say over where it goes. This is the true definition of Judas!

Do you think Mary got her three hundred pence worth? Why or why not? (I would love for you to email me your response and for you to post them to the video clip link on YouTube.)

I believe Mary got repaid to the fullest degree possible. Jesus already had given her Lazarus back, saved her soul, and granted her heaven. I think that payment was given in blessing while she lived on Earth. Moreover, at this dinner you had the twelve disciples, Mary, Martha, Lazarus, Simon, and his family. All of these family members and disciples were grateful to Jesus for healing them and giving them a new life. I can't image the worship and spiritual high in the room. This meeting was true, as high as it possible, as it could go on Earth. In addition, if this story is used to preach the death, burial, and resurrection of Christ then I believe that it was money well spent.

Verse 22-25 we are going to cover in another class. The Holy Spirit has taught me much about the meaning of the bread and where it come from in the Old Testament. Our focus today would be abandoned if we go there now. Please read the following passage again:

26 And when they had sung an hymn, they went out into the mount of

Olives. My question to you is: "How important are hymns? Are Hymns and Praise and Worship different?

_____

_____

_____

    I'd like to examine the following verse: **Colossians 3:16** Let the message of Christ dwell among you richly as you teach and admonish one another with all wisdom through psalms, hymns, and songs from the Spirit, singing to God with gratitude in your hearts. This scripture says, that God gives talents to all who love him. He gives us songs, hymns, and poems to edify Himself and to teach His people. What I do notice is not just one of the twelve or people in the room singing alone while everyone else is listening. I haven't read a scripture that tells me that Lazarus stood up and sang solo. However, I'm not saying solos are bad, but I'm saying we are all required to sing. The following scriptures prove that we are not only to listen to songs, but we are all supposed to sing to God.

> **Psalm 33:1-3**
>
> Sing for joy in the LORD, O you righteous ones; Praise is becoming to the upright. Give thanks to the LORD with the lyre; Sing praises to Him with a harp of ten strings. Sing to Him a new song; Play skillfully with a shout of joy.
>
> **Psalm 96:1-2**
>
> Sing to the LORD a new song; Sing to the LORD, all the earth. Sing to the LORD, bless His name; Proclaim good tidings of His salvation from day to day.

Psalm 5:11

But let all who take refuge in You be glad, Let them ever sing for joy; And may You shelter them, That those who love Your name may exult in You.

Psalm 9:11

Sing praises to the LORD, who dwells in Zion; Declare among the peoples His deeds.

Therefore, while we are in the congregation we are to sing to the Lord. We do not need to think about who is listening other than Jesus. In the Bible the command of singing is praise. Never let our congregational singing pass with nonchalant singing. Singing on a daily basis has changed my life! Singing with my family has also grown us closer together. This has given me a more spirit filled life. I would like for you to ponder a bit longer here by answering the following question: What songs do you know the best? Is it the most recent songs on the radio or the songs from your youth?

_____

_____

_____

Why?

_____

_____

_____

I've been a teacher, by trade, for some time. I have a BS, MA, and almost a doctorate degree in education. I've also surveyed many folks using the above question. Almost, every one of them as told me that they love the songs from their youth and they know them best. So, if we love the songs of our youth, why then do most people, allow their children to listen to songs of destruction? The best church singer I ever knew was self-taught! She never had one music lesson! She learned how to sing from going, three days a week, to church as a child; and now as she is almost a grandmother. Just to reiterate the obvious, note what **Proverbs 22:6** tells us!

One of the last things, I want to point out; is that public school systems are not teaching choir to every student. If we want edifying music to continue; then, we must foster it! People that attend churches who have no songs books, because they want to be "new age" are missing the mark, a bit! Churches that sing from the song book and pass on the knowledge of how to follow along; are actually more advanced. Their children can carry a tune and tell the difference between just lyrics and the chorus. Therefore, we must follow the example of Jesus and His disciples and sing hymns.

THE ANOINTING OF JESUS ACCORDING TO LUKE

Questions:

1. Who was the woman who anointed Jesus feet!
2. Why was spikenard the choice of ointment?
3. How would spikenard have benefited Jesus?

Please turn with me to **Luke 7:36-49**! Some, say that this account is the same one mentioned in Matthew and John, but Luke gives different details. Luke reports that Jesus and his 12 disciples have been invited to Simon's house for dinner.

This Simon is a Pharisee. Luke tells us that he lives in the city and a lady that lives in the city has heard about the dinner and wishes to attend. This biblical truth, takes place in the town of Bethany. According to Scripture, we are having a dinner party. In Jesus's time and currently, in the Middle East, parties that sit down and eat together are known to be friends. For example, if you look at pictures of our government officials, you'll notice that they never are eating together. In the middle east, eating together is very significant. You'll never find a Middle Eastern eating with an enemy.

I can imagine that this is a "set up" for Jesus from the Pharisees. Often, in the culture of that time, they would have Harlots and prostitutes, come dance for them. This Mary was a sinner, but she had access to the Pharisees home. Therefore, we can confer that the Pharisee helped her in her sinning endeavors. On the other hand, in this culture, it was often that uninvited people could enter the dining room, but they had to stand along the side of the wall. In any case, there was a woman at this dinner and she truly stopped the meal to worship Jesus.

A woman in this time period was not allowed to touch a man. Certainly, she would not have been permitted to touch a Rabbi/Profit like Jesus. Moreover, I like the fact that everyone was stunned to see a woman in the room, close to the dinner table, and touching the guest. In addition to touching the guest she even left her bodily fluids (tears) on Him. Then she used her hair to dry his feet, and then she kissed his feet. Finally, I notice here, that Jesus did not seem to have the same beliefs as the other men in the room. Jesus embraced the woman, allowed contact, and publicly praised her. Jesus broke down all the cultural rules for women in these scriptures.

The Lady in this occurrence, came to Pharisees house with a pure heart for Jesus. Scripture does not tell us why the lady attended the party. Scripture only tells us that she was a sinner. It is truly possible that the Pharisees arranged her to be there to entice Jesus to break a law, so, they legally would have a reason to cast Him in prison or kill him. -But the woman had a different plan.

Was Simon the Pharisee for Jesus or against Jesus?

To locate the answer Re-read verse 40. Jesus says, "Simon, I have something to say to you. When I entered your home, you did not greet me with a kiss, nor did you give me any water for my feet, and thirdly, you did not give me any perfume." It was possible that everyone who came for he was invited for the dinner received these basic gestures of kindness. From these actions, we can conclude that Simon did not like Jesus and was not one of God's people.

Today, when a guest arrives at your home, you should offer to take their coat. Next, offer them something to eat and drink. This would be the bare minimum of hospitality. In the days of this dinner, their custom was first to offer a kiss on each check. Then, the guests unfastened their shoes and a water basin with lavender was provided to wash their feet. Then, pure oil was offered as a perfume for their head and neck. Simon offered none of those to Jesus. It is possible that everyone else got this treatment except Jesus. How would you like to visit my home and I took everyone's coat? Then, gave them water and a snack, but purposely left you out? Would you even have stayed for dinner?

_____

_____

_____

Notice, the Scripture that states the sinner broke the alabaster box. You or I may have opened the box. However, if we open the perfume we would also have ability to close the perfume. Mary (the sinner) had no intent of holding anything back from Jesus. On the other hand, we come to church or we come in contact with our families and our heart is just broken. We may mask it for a short while, but eventually the tears began to flow, and the story is brought to life. This is a picture of the box that's broken, because it symbolizes her broken heart. How many times have we come to Jesus with a broken heart? How many times has the world disappointed us? How many times has the very elect discourage us from obeying God? How many times has life just left you with a broken heart?

Luke tells us, the woman falls at Jesus's feet! This was total radical behavior for this time period. Her actions were even seen as unbecoming of a woman. This woman had no head covering and had no veil, but she was in the presence of the Lord. Sometimes, when we come in the presence of the lord we may not be able to control our emotions. We may have to jump-up, testify, sing a song, shout, run the aisles, or fall on our knees. She loved Jesus with all of her heart, body, and soul. She loved Jesus so much she wanted to give him all that she owed. What would you be willing to give your child or your parents?

_____

Scripture says if your child asks for a loaf of bread, you're not going to give them a rock, but the whole loaf. (**Matthew 7:9**)

How many times have you been in a room and you're the only woman or the only person of a certain race. Are you comfortable? _____ Do you become so loud that you become the main focus of the group or do you stay more in the back ground? Why or why not? (**Ecclesiastes 3:1**)

_____

_____

_____

She wanted to bless Jesus. She may have even wondered if everyone in the room knew who was in the room. Perhaps, she thought everyone should be embracing Him with the same love she was giving.

When you love someone, you will give them all that you have. Not half of it, but all of it. For example, I've seen married couples keep their finances totally separate, because they are stingy and controlling. These marriages are the ones in trouble. We should want to give our spouse what we have, because we love them. This woman wasn't stingy she wanted to warship the Lord. She broke the box and had no intentions of reserving it!

Current research/uses for Myrrh?

Researchers have become interested in myrrh due to its potent antioxidant activity and potential as a cancer treatment. It has also been shown to be effective in fighting certain types of parasitic infections.

Myrrh's oil benefits! (from my experience and research)

- Fragrance
- Embalming
- Flavoring for food
- Treating **hay fever**
- As an antiseptic to clean and treat wounds
- As a paste to help stop bleeding
- Mouth wash (Bacteria Remover)

The smell of myrrh has been traditionally seen as a symbol of suffering, burned at funerals or other solemn events. But, at times myrrh is blended with citrus oils to help produce a more uplifting aroma. These lighter blends have been used to help promote inspiration and emotional insight.

THE ANOINTING OF JESUS ACCORDING TO JOHN.

Please decipher John chapter 12. Commencing on the first verse, the scripture expresses that this event occurred six days before Passover Jesus. When He arrived at Bethany He was met by the siblings: Lazarus, Martha, and Mary.

(We all know the story of Lazarus being raised from the dead.)

Teachers Note:

If you are in a group study review this before you proceed. For individual study record he main points.

— But to Jog your memory, I would like to convey the following:

Lazarus was all Mary and Martha had for a provider.

With Lazarus gone how would these women survive? In ancient times, women had no rights. Women were looked upon as dogs. The two sisters were truly devastated. Jesus heard of his dear friend being sick, but He for-knew the plan. Jesus was going to prove that the resurrection was real.

As soon as Martha seen Jesus she ran to meet Him in the field. She was Distraught and questioned Jesus on why did he not come sooner. Then, along came Mary and she questioned Jesus with the same question, why did you not come sooner? Then, the people in the room comforting Mary and Martha followed them and in their hearts they also questioned, "why did He not come sooner." Evidently, they did not hear about the earlier resurrection in a far-off village. However, the Jews did know of the blind man that had his sight restored. So, some of the people were angry, some were bitter, and some did not understand.

Then, Jesus asked Mary to take Him to the grave. Reluctantly Mary obliged. As they came close to the entrance Jesus requested the grave to be opened. I can only imagine the thought of someone asking me to open my brother's grave. My temperance sure would not be pleasing. Finally, scripture reports, that Jesus was filled with compassion and He calls Lazarus to come forward. What dismay? What excitement? What unbelief? Oh, what immediate reaction would we get if a loved one came out of the grave?

Anyway, Mary and Martha can be described as the ladies' fellowship leaders. These ladies could also be compared to the women at church that seem to always be there. The women who are always willing to serve the church with meals, fellowship, and prayer. The woman who are gifted with the gift of hospitality. For example, we know that they lived in Bethany near Jerusalem. Jerusalem was the capitol. Jesus often stopped by their house for Mary's cooking. Sometimes, He arrived with his twelve disciples, and the family was so gracious to feed everyone. You could say, Jesus was a frequent flyer at their house, but we know there were no airplanes.

As the custom, many other Jews could have also been there. I don't believe that the Sadducees and the Pharisees were there. In fact, they were brought to the site later. Like today, that would be like us having the government over for dinner. This just doesn't happen! The Sadducees and the Pharisees were concerned about the Jews, because they had quit going to the synagogue and started following Jesus around. Therefore, Jesus had to do God's work in secret.

The Sadducees and Pharisees were not concerned about the wellbeing of anyone, but maybe Judas! It comes down to greed, gain, and tithing. Some folks in the mist were concerned about meeting Jesus and learning from Him. However, some people could have been there, because they wanted to see Lazarus. A majority of the Jews believed his miracle was a hoax. Others could have been in search of Lazarus, because they wanted to put him to death. Finally, some folks were there to truly worship and fellowship with Jesus.

Passover Review:

Passover was celebrated because, God took His children out of the slavery in Egypt! They were celebrating the remembrance of the great escape from Egypt. God's death Angel passed over them. (In the book of Hebrews, the angle was named The Destroyer.) This celebration ensures that the story was passed down to their children and children's children.

The family of Mary, Martha, and Lazarus adored Jesus. We can see that they loved him by their actions. However, Mary brought their worship to a totally different level. She used their most prized family heirloom. This ointment (essential oil) could have been used for so many different reasons. Yet, they used it to worship Jesus.

- So far, have you thought beyond the monetary value and health we have discussed? The Lord pointed out another mystery to me. To explain this mystery, answer the following questions!

What kind of faith does it take for a person to give up their medicine?

_____

Today, would you give Christ your medicine?

_____

Are you totally sold out to Jesus and The Father?

_____

Do you believe your every need will be fulfill?

_____

Oil is spiritually important! God chose His profits by pouring on the oil. This signaled to His people that this person was filled with the spirit of the Lord. We often forget that Jesus is the oil in our lamp vessel. We are anointed with the oil (The Holy Spirit) and now have powers this world can't control. Mary, Martha, and Lazarus physically seen and felt the power of God. They were totally sold-out to Jesus. Their faith was fulfilled when they saw Lazarus become sick, die, and be raised again. They knew that the oil's spiritual meaning outweighed the monetary value. They proved their faith when she emptied the vessel on the body of Jesus. Mary knew that she did not need the healing onement, because she had the ultimate healer!

Re-read the above paragraph! I believe this is the entire point, to all the books, the Holy Spirit has given me. In the space record the message.

_____

_____

_____

I know we could stop with the lesson after that last paragraph, but the Holy Spirit me another message. Therefore, turn your thoughts again to The Word. Does the Word not warn us that evil is very close to us? Judas was a true wolf in sheep's clothing. He truly walked with the 12 apostles, dressed in like manner, kept the same mannerisms, and in fact, he was the groups treasure. However, Judas was a thief by trade. He skimmed a little from the top and concealed his identity very well. Notice, scripture reports that he knew exactly how much the essential oil was worth in monetary value. I'm sure, he also knew the medical value. He was not interested in helping anyone. He was interested in filling his pockets. Moreover, Judas was not part of the 12, because he loved Jesus. Judas was part of the 12 apostles, because he was interested in gaining power and wealth! He thought Jesus was going to be the king of the Jews. He believed that he would be rewarded in God's Earthly Kingdom.

During this time in Jewish history there were four major political divisions. The political divisions were divided into the Pharisees, Sadducees, Essences, and the Zealots. The Pharisees were in love with the law. The members of the Pharisees were priests and scribes. Not only the law of Moses, but also the laws they created. They wanted everyone to keep the laws of Moses and their new laws. The Sadducees were the wealthy Jews. They wanted everyone to study God word; while, keeping the Romans happy. The Zealots, which is the group Judas came from, wanted to end Roman rule. Historians call the Zealots the first terrorist, because they believed they were justified in all their works even if it meant breaking the ten commandments. In addition, I have read other accounts that believe Judas came from Kerioth.

Review and complete the chart with the information you learned. Later, when you are reviewing the information it will be clearly marked for you.

Political Parties	Describe the groups focus.
1.	
2.	
3.	
4.	

Kerioth is in southern Judea. All of the other apostles were Galilean. Politically, Galilee was a neutral area. All of these groups believed there would be a Messiah coming to build a kingdom. They all looked for a deliverer. However, Jesus upset all of them, because he sided with no political parties. (**Luke 17:20-21**)

Can you pinpoint a Judas in your environment?

_____

_____

_____

(If you are teaching this lesson spend some time here. Listen and allow everyone to react.)

I would declare that there are a lot of false profits in Christian circles today. I would also adventure to affirm there are a lot of people portraying a Christian life but interested only in making a profit. Anytime, someone new joins your group you need to pray and ask for discernment. Although, blindly trusting the leaders of your church, is not good either. Today, we can't trust just everyone. When someone speaks (even if you have known them all your life) you need to check out their story. Sometimes, like Judas people are very good at hiding the truth and their motives.

In summation, I'd like for you to consider the books in the gospels again! We realize the woman showed a style of sacrificial worship. This is the true focus of this scripture. God, reminds us that life is so much more than just living for ourselves. He calls us for a greater purpose. He uses this woman to show us how to live a sacrificial life and to reassure us that He is all we need. We should live our daily lives sacrificing for Jesus. On the other hand, we should be looking around at other people; for the purpose of intervening on their behalf. Our decision to intervene should not be based on their merit, because God did not save us based on our merit. Sometimes, we have too much stuff, sometimes we have too much stuff to do, and sometimes we look out for ourselves, but Scripture teaches us here that we need to look beyond ourselves and help our friends, family, neighbors.

THE MESSAGE OF THE MYRTLE TREE!

Have you ever heard of the Myrtle Tree?

_____

_____

_____

Have you ever seen a Myrtle Tree?

_____

_____

_____

Myrtle is an evergreen flowering shrub that initiated from Africa, but has become a native plant in the Mediterranean region. This plant is petite in size, contains opaque green leaves, blossoms with purple-black colored berries, and delivers a fragrant aroma. Harvesters today remove oil from the leaves. The oil from berries is often used as a flavoring agent for beverages and sat alone to be used as a juice.

Uses for Myrtle

According to the **Bible**, it was used in purification ceremonies.
In other **cultures**, the essential oil of myrtle was used to help ease urinary infections, digestive issues and respiratory illnesses.
Greek physicians used the plant oil for lung and bladder infections, while in Italy, the oil was an ingredient in children's cough syrup.
Romans: The oil found in myrtle leaves was also used in skincare and as a remedy to regulate menstrual cycles.

What Spiritual connections does the Myrtle Tree have for us? (Take a stab at the answer. Then, return after you complete this lesson and write down your learnings)-This is another technique I use to teach youngers to check their comprehension?

_____

_____

_____

Perhaps, you have heard of the Myrtle tree. If you live in Oregon, you know all about it. I know you've read it in scripture, but most of us just read over minute details. This is when we miss some of the most valuable information. To understand a literary work, you must understand the context in which it was written. The Bible is no different! Hopefully, you find this to be true! I believe that teaching Biblical content is my current purpose!

God wants saturated the entire land of Judea with myrtle trees. Myrtle trees need a very rich soil to prosper. In the Middle East, the tree never loses its leaves. In the United States the tree is kind of like an evergreen tree. The blooms of this tree flowers into giant-sized white flowers. These white flowers bloom in the Spring and contain an amazing aroma. Jews believed that white meant purity and if you were pure you were also clean. The word clean means to be absolved of sin and immortality would be your reward. They also knew purple was the color of royalty and spender. In ancient times, women would often dry these flowers and use them in their homes for potpourri. They would also make necklaces and bracelets for both the wrists and the ankle.

On a side note; Queen Easter's name in Hebrew means Myrtle. Like Lavender, Myrtle is a soft essential oil. The word soft means mild. The mildness/meekness of this essential oil permitted for the common use of this oil. Many people today admit that Myrtle essential oil is a staple in their homes. It is such a soft essential oil that it can be rubbed on the skin of even a newborn; therefore, adults use Myrtle essential oil as a skin softener.

We also find the mention of Myrtle in Scripture around six times. According to Nehemiah chapter 8 the Myrtle bloom was used during the feast of Tabernacles. This is one of the four plants blessed by the Lord. You see, to be used during this feast, a plant had to have three leaves and grown from one point. What do you think that symbolizes?

_____

_____

_____

Of course, it does! The Trinity of, God the Father, Jesus Christ, and the Holy Spirit. What is The Feast of Tabernacles?

_____

_____

_____

This was the last feast of the year. It was done about harvest time; therefore, it is also known as the harvest gathering. For eight days, Jews would gather, build temporary tents, and live outside. This was to remind them of the time God's people spent in the wilderness. Trusting God by moving their people by the cloud in the day and fire by in the night.

Now, since we have discussed a few details of Jewish history. Let's turn to the book of Zachariah. This book can be located by turning to Matthew and then carefully turn back two chapters. Then, you'll find the book of Zachariah. The book of Zachariah is perhaps one of the most refreshing books of the Old Testament. Most of the books found in the Old Testament convey judgment, but Zachariah brought words of comfort to God's people.

Zachariah wrote his chapter after their exile from slavery. The world was at rest, because Persia had concurred all the territories. Much like today, our world is at rest, but trouble continues to surface. Wars and rumors of war abound. The red horse and man that stands in the middle represents Jesus. Jesus is standing in the mist of all who love him. Jesus is not afar off looking down at His people, but He is in the low place with his people. He has brought His angles to encompass them. Just like today, Jesus offers His protection, and secures it with His angelic beings.

Zachariah explains his vision with this perfect picture. His people are experiencing hay and stubble. There, world and property are heavily damaged. Life seems to be unrepairable! The people are depressed and see no light at the end of the tunnel. But then, God reveals His plan through this chosen vessel. God reminds His people that He will never leave or forsake them. He is always in control and with Him all things are possible. Finally, within the next couple of years, the temple is rebuilt, and the people are once again prosperous.

Fir essential oil

Class Script

Today's Scriptures:

1 Kings 6:34

_____

_____

_____

34 And the two doors were of fir tree: the two leaves of the one door were folding, and the two leaves of the other door were folding.

1 Kings 9:11

_____

_____

_____

(Now Hiram the king of Tyre had furnished Solomon with cedar trees and fir trees, and with gold, according to all his desire,) that then king Solomon gave Hiram twenty cities in the land of Galilee.

2 Kings 19:23

_____

_____

_____

By thy messengers thou hast reproached the LORD, and hast said, With the multitude of my chariots I am come up to the height of the mountains, to the sides of Lebanon, and will cut down the tall cedar trees thereof, and the choice fir trees thereof: and I will enter the lodgings of his borders, and into the forest of his Carmel.

2 Chronicles 2:8

_____

_____

_____

Send me also cedar trees, fir trees, and algum trees, out of Lebanon: for I know that thy servants can skill to cut timber in Lebanon; and, behold, my servants shall be with thy servants,

2 Chronicles 3:5

_____

_____

_____

And the greater house he sealed with fir tree, which he overlaid with fine gold, and set thereon palm trees and chains.

Psalms 104:17

_____

_____

_____

Where the birds make their nests: as for the stork, the fir trees are her house.

Isaiah 14:8

_____

_____

_____

Yea, the fir trees rejoice at thee, and the cedars of Lebanon, saying, since thou art laid down, no feller is come up against us.

Isaiah 37:24

_____

_____

_____

By thy servants hast thou reproached the Lord, and hast said, By the multitude of my chariots am I come up to the height of the mountains, to the sides of Lebanon; and I will cut down the tall cedars thereof, and the choice fir trees thereof: and I will enter into the height of his border, and the forest of his Carmel.

Isaiah 41:19

_____

_____

_____

I will plant in the wilderness the cedar, the shittah tree, and the myrtle, and the oil tree; I will set in the desert the fir tree, and the pine, and the box tree together:

Isaiah 55:13 (Read two different versions of scripture and record the differences in the space provided.)

_____

_____

_____

Instead of the thorn shall come up the fir tree, and instead of the brier shall come up the myrtle tree: and it shall be to the LORD for a name, for an everlasting sign that shall not be cut off.

Isaiah 60:13

_____

_____

_____

The glory of Lebanon shall come unto thee, the fir tree, the pine tree, and the box together, to beautify the place of my sanctuary; and I will make the place of my feet glorious.

Ezekiel 27:5

_____

_____

_____

They have made all thy ship boards of fir trees of Senir: they have taken cedars from Lebanon to make masts for thee.

Ezekiel 31:8

_____

_____

_____

The cedars in the garden of God could not hide him: the fir trees were not like his boughs, and the chestnut trees were not like his branches; nor any tree in the garden of God was like unto him in his beauty.

Hosea 14:8

_____

_____

_____

Ephraim shall say, what have I to do any more with idols? I have heard him, and observed him: I am like a green fir tree. From me is thy fruit found.

Nahum 2:3

_____

_____

_____

The shield of his mighty men is made red, the valiant men are in scarlet: the chariots shall be with flaming torches in the day of his preparation, and the fir trees shall be terribly shaken.

Zechariah 11:2

_____

_____

_____

Howl, fir tree; for the cedar is fallen; because the mighty are spoiled: howl, O ye oaks of Bashan; for the forest of the vintage is come down.

The best way to describe the fir tree is to picture our modern-day Christmas Tree.

Fir essential oil scent reminds me of the smell of Christmas. The aroma is fresh and crisp, but woody. For this reason, Fir can be described as having a very masculine smell. The smell of Fir is the opposite of a flower.

When you think of Christmas what pops in your mind first! I hope's it's not presents!

_____

_____

_____

For the true and only meaning of Christmas read Mathew Chapter 2.

What say you?

_____

_____

_____

In biblical days, the most popular tree was the fir tree. Since the biblical people used it like pine, scholars believe fir really was pine. People knew where to find the trees. God taught his people how to use the trees. The use of the trees improved their standard of living. The men used it as cologne to attract the women. The most famous tribe of Fir trees were found in Lebanon.

Teachers Note: At this point in the lesson present essential oils like Douglas fir and Cedar! Remove the cap from the lid and pass the essential oil around the room. While the oil is circulating be sure to tell the class/group any personal interactions you have had or have witnessed. You may also include a handout explaining the benefits.

Example One: The price of Douglas fir is very reasonable, because it's North America's most plentiful softwood species. Douglas fir is about one fifth of the U.S.'s total softwood reserves.

Example Two: Herbalist love the antiseptic resin we obtained from the trunk. It is used to treat cuts, burns, wounds and other skin ailments. Recently, my daughter, Elianna, had a cough and sore throat. We used the essential oil in two ways. First, we put the diffuser in her room and put 5 drops of the oil in water. We ran the diffuser constantly! This lessoned her cough. **Next,** we made her chew on some of the leaves in an effort to help her throat. Of course, the doctor claimed she had strip throat, but we claim God's medicine gave her comfort.

Example two, some of my Native American friend's state, they infuse the oil and green bark to treat symptoms of their menstruation and bleeding bowels. It was also reported to me that the oils and leaves placed in a warm bathe, helps with arthritis and paralyzed joints.

On a side note: please inform your audience of a lesson in volume one that talks about how God created us all different; therefore, the essential oils in this book, may react on people differently. You can further state that a person should never try to use any essential oils that they are allergic to.

Record the following verse in your own words if you did not do so at the beginning of the lesson. If you have already done so, then just answer the question to the best of your ability.

In **Isaiah 60:13** what was made from the fir/pine tree?

_____

_____

_____

According to **Hosea 14:8**, What type of trees were they?

_____

_____

_____

In **1 Kings 6:15** we learn what they used the trees to make. What were they used to create?

_____

_____

_____

In **1 Kings 9:11** what was King Solomon building?

_____

_____

_____

How about **Ezekiel 27:5**, what did the people create?

_____

_____

_____

What is recorded in **2 Samuel 6:5**? What David use the wood to create?

_____

_____

_____

_____

In **Nahum 2:3** how did God's people use the fir tree?

_____

_____

_____

In **2 Chronicles 2:8** what was created?

_____

_____

_____

Finally, in **2 Chronicles 3:5** how was the fir tree used?

_____

_____

_____

From the scripture above we can see how God taught his people to use the tree. God always gives us more than what we deserve and need. We could survive living in tents and other structures, but we see here God wanted better for his people. If not, he would have keep this a secret from his people. Today, you can distill the oil from fir trees through their sap, needles and twigs, from the trunk, and by collecting sap from the outside of the tree- around the bark.

Below is a picture of the process to help you visualize how ancient people obtained the oil.

Let's examine the imagery the people of the bible used to convey to its readers! Re-read your introduction verses. Let's examine the imagery the people of the bible used to convey to its readers!

But first, what is a metaphor? On the space below provide the definition.

_____

_____

_____

Basically understood a metaphor describes a person, place, or thing; then, it is combined with an interesting or imagery expression. Such as "KNOWING IS SEEING" or "TIME IS MOTION"

The Bible uses metaphors to create a clearer meaning of the topics it addresses. To understand the Bible clearer it's imperative that we understand the diverse types of metaphors and how they are used in the Bible. Today, we still use metaphors in an attempt to get someone else to understand our ideas.

For the verses below record what you feel the images represent!

Psalms 104:17

_____

_____

_____

The imagery in this verse are found in more than the location the birds and where the birds make their nests. Where do they nest?

_____

_____

_____

God did not want you to only know that, but with his wisdom he wanted us to know that what He does for the bird he will do for us.

In the questions here, what else can we learn about the birds? I provided you with some questions you can investigate. (I have also written a book about birds of the bible — You may want to study)

1. Who taught the birds: Where to nest? For what reasons, did they need the nest?

    _____

    _____

    _____

2. Who taught the birds when to build their nests? (hint seasons)

    _____

_____

_____

_____

3. Who showed them how to build the nest?

_____

_____

_____

4. What do birds use to create the perfect nest?

_____

_____

_____

5. Did an architect show the birds their blueprint?

_____

_____

_____

6. Did the birds pluck their own feathers for their nest? Did they learn from their mothers that this would create a soft bed for their children? Who oversees the birds?

7. Who provides the birds with nourishment?

_____

_____

_____

8. Who taught them to sing?

_____

_____

_____

9. Why do they sing?

_____

_____

_____

10. Who provides the bird of the birds?

_____

_____

_____

11. Who adds to the number of the birds?

_____

_____

_____

Isaiah 14:8

_____

_____

_____

In this verse the people of Biblical days realized the importance of not destroying God's creation. Something we should mandate by law, because society have turned from God's way. Our people are so full of greed. Losing the ability to destroy would hurt some of their pocketbooks. We should take this as a warning to watch how we are treating God's world. In addition, both the people and the forest are rejoicing, because the king of Babylon can no longer cut down the forest for his benefit.

Isaiah 55:13

_____

_____

_____

We see here in Isaiah that the land was laying in waste. The once thriving "happy" land is now full of thorns and briers. The throne represents sin in the bible! Now; however, God has restored his people. The fir tree in the bible represented life, greatness, and joy; therefore, we see in this verse God's promise to be with Israel forever and they will have peace with God.

Ezekiel 31:8

_____

_____

_____

The scriptures report kingdoms as being like the distinct types of trees. Israel being like fir trees- restored. While the other kingdoms appear rich; however, their pride will surely make them fall. Heaven is our goal! Its trees will be nothing like what we see in our environment.

Hosea 14:8

_____

_____

_____

Hosea is communicating to his readers that God is the true tree of Life and that it is an honor to look upon Him. Hosea, is most likely referring to the trees of Lebanon, because these were the most precious and expensive trees. Everyone and every nation wanted to own the massive trees of Lebanon. However, this author can find nothing in her research to state exactly what tree he was referring too. Regardless, of the tree and where he was located; the meaning for us, is that we should not forget our provider. We should never take our blessings and positions for granted. We should especially not overlook the ones we don't notice every day. We want to remind ourselves and God how thankful we are for what He has allowed us to obtain.

An additional lesson within this lesson follows: (Part 2)

The Israelites spent 40 days and 40 nights in the wilderness. How much food do you think it would take to feed 2 to 3,000,000 people, a day?

_____

_____

_____

How much water do you think they would need in the desert to survive?

_____

_____

_____

How has God provided you with your needs?

_____

_____

_____

In the following box add ten things that the Lord provided for you. Then, put them in the back of the Bible so when you need encouragement you can refer to your list.

Not only did these birds deliver food right in front of the door, but The Master provided it! The amount of food one army general in charge of nutrition, stated, that was needed for one day, would be about two freight trains full. Then, a freight train of water! Furthermore, God's children lived in the desert. They had no stoves or ovens. Therefore, what would have been needed to cook and prepare their food? The army general, estimated that another freight train of wood would have been needed.

We can learn from this experience in Scripture. Did you catch the spiritual meaning of the cloud by morning and fire by night?

_____

_____

_____

God's children were being taught several lessons. In summation, the children followed God, He provided, and He made the way. I hope that the Spirit reveals to you that we shall follow Christ. Friend, when there is no way God will make away. Don't be faint in spirit our God will provide.

GOD WILL PROVIDE.

Please read **2 Kings 4:1-7**. This chapter describes the events of Elisha. Elisha performed four miracles. These miracles were not of his will, but the will of the Father. These miracles, prove that God loves and cares for his faithful children. In questions 1-4 explain the miracles Elisha performed.

1. **2 Kings 4:1-7**

_____

_____

_____

2. **2 Kings 4:32-37**

_____

_____

_____

3. **2 Kings 4:38-41**

_____

_____

_____

4. **2 Kings 4:42-44**

_____

_____

_____

We will focus on account one, because it verifies the importance of essential oil. This account's sitting takes place at a widow's house. After drawing a map with these four events, I believe that the lady lives in Mount

Carmel. Mt. Carmel is near the sea of Galilee. Plus, Elisha lives near Jerusalem. Jerusalem is near the dead sea. According, to this chapter Elisha was moving south.

This lady was desperate and grieving. Her husband had died and left unpaid bills; therefore, the people he owed money too were going to take the widows two sons. This trade off, was a widespread practice in her day. The sons would have to work to pay the debt of the family. I could not image losing my husband and then losing my sons. How horrible? God's law was that every seventh year all the bondsman's and debtors would go free, but this rarely happened. People, just like today, were greedy! They did not always obey God. Read **Jeremiah 34:14** to confirm my statements above. Now that we understand, the widow truly had no place to turn let's move on. But then, God provided. She found Elisha. She reminded Elisha of her husband and told him of his good works. (v.1) After that speech, she explained her dilemma. Then, as a good servant of God, Elisha asks her how he could help. The widows answer explains her conditions. "I have nothing, but a little oil." To remind you of a more commonly reported account turn to **1 Kings 17:8-16**! What did Elisha provide that came from God?

The fact that scripture reports a pot tells us that this oil may be some type of cooking oil. (v 2) However, it is clear that this oil, was the family's savings. Often, we have a locked safe or a little money put aside for a rainy day. This oil was her rainy-day fund. In fact, **Proverbs 21:20** tells us to put oil aside for this type of day. Furthermore, knowing this scripture, ensures that this family has retained their faith. Throughout the Bible we see that God provides for the poor. He realizes that there will always be the poor. (**Matthew 26:11**) God often uses people to accomplish His goal. In this account He uses Elisha but read **Nehemiah 5:1-3**. How did God use Nehemiah?

In verse three, Elisha gives the widow the directions from God. As reported, the widow and her family travel to the homes of nearby neighbors. I can't image how many they gathered, but I'm sure God prepared the hearts of all who were involved. Notice here that the containers they gathered could have been very heavy! There were no recycled plastic products. The products may have been large water pots or something small like a tea cup. One thing is for sure they gathered plenty! Today, all essential oils are kept in dark glass. The jars are not cheap. When you give oil away it is a small sacrifice. Often, you never see the container again.

In the next verse, we are informed that the widow and her family went into the house and closed the door. This is signified! Locate the following scriptures and make a notation of what miracle was performed.

1 Kings 17:17-24 _____

2 Kings 4:38-41 _____

Jonah 2:1-10 _____

John 11:38 _____

Why do you think the family went into the house alone?

_____

_____

_____

According to the Webster's dictionary, a side show is described as follows: "a minor or diverting incident or issue, especially one that distracts attention from something more important." God must view all the aide He provides to His people as necessary, but not His priority. This is the same for us. Do we not want salvation before health? Is eternal life not the goal of this life?

Essential oils can replace the herbs and spices we use in our kitchens. They are safe! We have been eating them unknowingly for years. The pictures below are labels that contain essential oils.

The main difference between essential oils and cooking oils is the fat content. Essential oils come from the roots and stems of the plant; whereas, cooking oil comes from the bud or blossoms of the plant. Another difference between the two oils is that cooking oil leaves a greasy feeling. Therefore, we use specific oils for cooking. For example, when I spray olive oil in a skillet it makes a slippery surface; which, makes stir frying easier and clean up better.

Now, we have to be careful with the oils that we put in recipes. Not all essential oils are equal. For example, most therapeutic grade oils may be consumed, but some at the grocery store may not be food safe. One day, I ran out of lemon essential oil. I use lemon oil for lots of reasons, but that particular day I wanted to use it as a water flavoring. I went to my local health food store and asked for lemon essential oil and what they gave me was not ready for consumption. I was absolutely shocked!

When purchasing essential oils you want to look for the following words: certified pure therapeutic grade (CPTG). This means that the essential oil is made from plants which are harvested in the area in which God planted them. They ate distilled or cold pressed.80% of all essential oils can be used in cooking.

I have speculated that the widow probably had a bit of olive oil. This is one of the most commonly used oils; which, would have turned a great profit. However, the Holy Land was also full of grape vineyards. Therefore, this oil also lines up with scripture. Both of these oils can be used in cooking and in oil lamps. Grape seed oil has a less greasy film. So, it would have been the best oil to us for cleaning and sanitization.

Essential oils have almost totally replaced all of the fresh and dry herbs in my kitchen. The essential oils are 300% the potency of both dry and fresh herbs. The essential oils last a lifetime if you store them in cool dark places. This has saved my family money.

When are creating a recipe that calls for fresh or dried herbs I use the one drop method. If the recipe calls for 1 teaspoon I dry herbs I use a toothpick to get a half of a drop. If the recipe calls for a tablespoon I use one drop of oil. I always put the drop of oil on a spoon and then add the oil to my recipe. If I don't I end up ruining my dish. Remember, that when essential are heated they lose some of their other properties. It is better to wait until the dishes almost complete before adding that flavorful drop. However, I have found in my Italian dinner's, that the spices need to simmer in the pot a little longer. When using oregano, thyme, rosemary, or basil be sure to allow extra time for simmering.

Jessie's Simple Kitchen Recipes
(Please see the YouTube Channel for the recipes in action.)

1. **Water Flavorings:**

Directions: One drop of oil per 16 ounces in a glass of water. Orange, Grapefruit, Lemon, or Tangerine

Health Benefits:

A single drop of orange and grapefruit essential oils can meet 100% of your daily requirement of Vitamin C, makes you look younger, helps eye health, and Vitamin C content which is required for producing collagen which, in turn, is responsible for keeping the tissues in your hair together.

Lemon essential oils help cells stay healthy which keeps you from getting sick, Good healthy cells halt the production of cancer, increase the alkalize in the blood which helps relieve pain, decreased drowsiness, and more mental energy.

Tangerine essential oil heal wounds, improves digestion, stops the absorption of cholesterol, absorbs the iron from the food, fights against arthritis, and it eases the movements in the bowel.

2. **Favorized Salt:** Find a 4-ounce resealable jar. Add two ounces of table salt. Then add one drop of each oil: Basil, Rosemary, and Black Pepper. Then stir and tighten jar.

Usage: I use this mixture on all my dishes instead of plain salt.

Health Benefits:

Rosemary:

Helps increase your blood flow. An increased blood flow will help improve your memory, help your hair grow, and keep you from getting blood clots. Rosemary also gets gases to come out of the body and boots your immune system helps. So, for me this is the perfect.

Basil: This oil treats nausea, motion sickness, indigestion, constipation, respiratory problems, and diabetes. Basil oil is also a good source of Vitamin A, magnesium, potassium, iron, and calcium.

Black Pepper: This oil helps relief the symptoms of the common cold, constipation, indigestion, anemia, impotency, muscular strains, dental disease, pyorrhea, and heart disease.

3. **Sweet Drizzle:** (fruit and veggies) Using a 4-ounce resealable glass jar. Add 2-ounces of all natural Honey, because it is more liquefied. Then add a ½ drop of cinnamon, 2 drops of orange, 1 drop of ginger, 1 drop of on guard, and 1 drop of cardamom.

Health Benefits:

Supports healthy immune and respiratory function, Protects against environmental threats, Supports the body's natural antioxidant defenses, Promotes healthy circulation, Energizing and uplifting aroma, Regenerates muscle energy, helps weight loss, and improves morning sickness.

4. **Salad Dressing:** Any glass container with lid or stopper. Add 2-ounces of olive oil, 1 ounce of cider vinegar, 1 teaspoon dry mustard, ½ teaspoon of salt, ½ teaspoon of our flavored salt recipe, 3 drops of lemon and 1 drop of oregano.

Health benefits:

Oregano supports the health of the immune system, kill the foodborne pathogen, and if you get the flu it helps your body to get rid of unwanted phlegm in your lungs.

Plus, all of the amazing health benefits from our favorized salt!

Jessie's List of Oils in her Kitchen				
	Rosemary	Ginger	Basil	
	Clove	Black Pepper	Lemon	
Cinnamon	Wild Orange	Peppermint	Lime	On-Guard

For more information visit: www.findinghealinginGodsbackyard.com

4 MEN WITH LEPROSY

Please read **2 Kings 7: 1-16!**

Who is the main focus of this event? _____

Chapter 5 passage eight connects with 2 kings, because God said you and your children will be leopard's. So, this kind of leprosy was a generational curse. This entire community we're leopards. They were cursed with a fatal skin disease. However, we have a loving God who cares and loves his children. Since I'm a teacher, I like to think of this account as a series of test do-overs. God gave them a make-up test. In my class at school I have often had children retake a test or write something over, because they got an unfavorable score the first time.

This event in scripture, the leopards were faced with a decision. What were the details of this re-test?

_____

_____

_____

One of the main decisions the ones with leprosy had to make is hide everything and get rich or turn everything over to the king; so, their people could eat.

Some examples in scripture are as follows: He retested Moses after forty years in the wilderness. God showed up in a burning bush and called him back into service.

1. Abraham and Sarah develop their own plan to have a baby, but that was not God's plan. Then, in God's time He gave them a retest.
2. God told Jonah to go to Nineveh and preach that judgment was at hand. Jonah decided to do the wrong thing. So, God gave him a re-test.

3. Peter got a re-test, because he said he would never deny Jesus, but he did three times.

Personally, I know I have made mistakes and often I've asked the Lord to give me another opportunity to do it right. On the other hand, we (meaning me also) need to do things over and over again until we learn from our mistakes.

Noticed these four leopard's were from a community ostracized by the Jews. They were in a quarantine unit, but this unit became family. We all have inner circles or we should. We should all be a help to one another. We should not be a freeloader or a hindrance. We should all try to bring something to the table.

For my finally point on this topic, I thought of these two questions:

How many men were at the gate? _____

What did they have in common?

_____

_____

_____

What does scripture communicate to us about not to walking with the Ungodly? (This section is for group discussion)

_____

_____

_____

Amos 3:3 - Can two walk together, except they be agreed?

1 Thessalonians 5:22

_____

_____

_____

Romans 16:17

_____

_____

_____

1 Timothy 6:20

O Timothy, guard what has been entrusted to you, avoiding worldly and empty chatter and the opposing arguments of what is falsely called "knowledge"—

_____

_____

_____

2 Timothy 2:16

_____

_____

_____

2 Timothy 2:23

But refuse foolish and ignorant speculations, knowing that they produce quarrels.

Titus 3:9

But avoid foolish controversies and genealogies and strife and disputes about the Law, for they are unprofitable and worthless.

1 Thessalonians 5:22 abstain from every form of evil.

Especially in the time of need we need our neighbors, our church family, and certainly you immediate family will come together to help each other.

What the leopards finally realized is that God was in control. The re-test for these leopards came when came to the camp of the Syrian army and was faced with all the splendor. As stated in todays scripture, God caused the army to become scared and they ran. They ate and gain strength! Then, according to scripture they took the news back to their kingdom. This was their legacy. The legacy for those leopards affected generations to come. Sometimes, our family curses can be lifted according to what we do or how we sin.

Elisha again prophesies in seven days. At the end of chapter 7 verse 17 just as Elisha predicted One was would be trampled over about by the multitude. This is the third time that someone got at the gate and died. Perhaps, because they did not get the message God gave them. God can reverse their Leprosy, but he could also provide them with so much more. He knows the plans He has for each one of us, says Jeremiah. Sometimes, we have to take the risk to find out what God has prepared for us.

Now, there are sometimes that we are to wait upon the Lord. For our next point, go get this scripture, Isaiah 40: 28-33. Now, read it and paraphrase it's meaning in the space provided.

_____

_____

_____

Amen! (The activity you just performed was the right move. To obtain knowledge one must lean on God, but one also must put themselves into action.) If God has given you all the tools, then it's your turn. Get off your knees, dust them off, and get to work!

Why Jesus can be called as a "Balm of Gilead"

Class Script

Teachers Note from book one:

The closest plant to the Tree of Gilead that we have alive today, is the state tree of Kansas. The state tree of Kansas is known as the Cottonwood Tree. This tree grows to six feet in diameter. The cottonwood tree is a part of the softwood tree family, because it blooms in the spring and the dead limbs need to be pruned in the Fall. People cut this tree down, because when the cotton falls off or is spread by the wind it sticks to everything. Mainly cars and walkways. The buds are grinded up when trodden down and forms a sticky paste. This sticky paste is annoying when trying to scrap it off sidewalk.

If people would harvest the cotton they could avoid the mess. Once, the buds are removed they could make a pain re-mover. The best buds come from the top of the tree, but others that fall can also be used. You crush these with rocks and apply directly to the wound. It also pushes out infection, helps with congestion, and coughs.

The balm of Gilead also was used in the same manner as we use the cottonwood tree. The balm of Gilead came from a Gilead tree in the land East of the Jordan. It was the land given to the tribes of Reuben and Gad. In Biblical times, a little balm was an aromatic plant retrieved from the gum of tree in Gilead. Scripture in Genesis states that the Ishmaelite traders purchased Joseph from his brothers, but were carrying this balm of Gilead to Egypt. The Egyptians used the buds, branches, and bark to treat chronic infections, cough, wounds, bruises, snake bite, and even sore throats. Although, I can't imagine it tasting great! Because, the Balm of Gilead was not syrupy. In fact, creating a syrup would have been very hard work.

Let's examine the following scriptures to examine the Gilead tree in more detail:

Genesis 37:25

25And they sat down to eat bread: and they lifted up their eyes and looked, and, behold, a company of Ishmaelites came from Gilead with their camels bearing spicery and balm and myrrh, going to carry it down to Egypt.

The balm is one of the fist ointments found in scripture. From all accounts the balm was an effective healing ointment for many indications. The people of the Bible distilled it from the eleo-resin of a tree.

Jeremiah 51:8

8 Babylon is suddenly fallen and destroyed: howl for her; take balm for her pain, if so be she may be healed.

It was apparently used for its pain-relieving capabilities. It was also known as the Balm of Mecca, The Balm of Jericho, and the Balm of Gilead.

Jeremiah 8:20

20The harvest is past, the summer is ended, and we are not saved.

Jeremiah 9:1 Oh that my head were waters, and mine eyes a fountain of tears, that I might weep day and night for the slain of the daughter of my people!

God questions His people. Why do you not return to me? How many seasons must pass. The harvest is coming, but there will be known found here in Gilead.

Genesis 43:11 11 And their father Israel said unto them, If it must be so now, do this; take of the best fruits in the land in your vessels, and carry down the man a present, a little balm, and a little honey, spices, and myrrh, nuts, and almonds:

This scripture we see the end of Joseph's story. Jacob sent his sons to Egypt to find food. Some of the other spices would have been poppy seed, pepper, coriander, mint, and marjoram.

Ezekiel 27:17

17Judah, and the land of Israel, they were thy merchants: they traded in thy market wheat of Minnith, and Pannag, and honey, and oil, and balm.

The Balm was hybrid. It required a skillful gardener to really flourish.

1 Kings 10:10 And she gave the king an hundred and twenty talents of gold, and of spices very great store, and precious stones: there came no more such abundance of spices as these which the queen of Sheba gave to king Solomon.

Queen Sheba visited King Solomon and provided him with a twig to grow his own garden.

(Note: In the first book we made a coat of many colors and discussed Joseph's story in great detail. You may want to stop here and re-visit this lesson.)

Ok, I hope you know how hard it is to create the balm into medicine. To recap, in book one, we discussed the cotton wood tree and the fig tree; therefore, processing this balm into a medicine would haven take a lot of grinding or baking in the sun. We can compare it with the love of Jesus. For Jesus to become a balm (ointment), He was smitten, bruised and beaten for our transgressions and iniquities. His precious blood was shed on the cross. Today, our faith in His blood in essence represents the balm. Millions of people who are sick physically and spiritually need cleansing on the inside look to "the balm" only Jesus can offer.

As we have examined the balm of Gilead we learned that it is a healing ointment. Now, we can compare this little bit of healing to understand that Jesus is a healer of all sicknesses. He is the Balm of Gilead. From the days of old we witnessed leopards healed, Blind eyes restored, and more. Today, we see Jesus heal every disease. In His blood man is healed of every critical health condition that exists and every sin sickness that abounds.

Jesus imputed our sin on himself. His blood flows through our veins. The Holy Spirt takes charge over your inner being. This action unleashes everlasting healing within you. Thus, we become new creatures that grow in Christ. Our old Adam is gone and a new sprout of living water flows.

The Balm of Gilead was created by God and is a free gift through Jesus. He is the source of all healing. He is the one who can set us free from all our iniquities. and fornication when we receive him as our Savior.

GROWING OLDER AND THE NEED FOR PRECIOUS OINTMENT.

CLASS SCRIPT

YouTube Video Arranged

(Note: In my first book, Finding Healing in God's Backyard, page 30-35, you'll find more information on the following examples.)

Everyone that is saved in their older age always wishes they would have accepted Him sooner, because they would have built a closer walk with Jesus. According to scriptures and our Elders, knowing God sooner would have given them a more abundant life. For example, money can't buy precious lessons taught my Christ. God created essential oils and taught his people how to use them. God even gave essential oils more significance (worth) by bringing them into the synagogue (church). From our youth, I believe we were supposed to know about God's medicine.

Side Note:

Scientist have found tombs of Kings and Queens with alabaster boxes full of oil. This fact, I hope, leads you to think about the importance of essential oils. Why would people want to be buried with it?

_____

_____

_____

God's people used essential oils from birth to death. They used these oils in every aspect of their life. Read the following scriptures and note how God's people used these oils.

Paraphrase the following scriptures:

John 19:40

_____

_____

_____

Genesis 24:32

_____

_____

_____

Exodus 30:22-25

_____

_____

_____

1 John 4:1

_____

_____

_____

Those are just a few examples! Myrrh essential oil is a commonly known oil, because of the Christmas story, and I want to use this as an example to explain God's gift to mankind. Myrrh fights against infections; therefore, when a baby was born the ambilocal cord was cut and treated with Myrrh. Then, during life myrrh was used for all sorts of reasons. A couple examples are in all the all the gospels and these scriptures record that Jesus went to the cross and He was offered vinegar to drink mingled with gall. Myrrh was often and still being used for pain relief. Finally, at the end of life

Myrrh essential oil was used for mummification. For example, a 100-pound mixture of myrrh and aloes was brought to wrap Jesus' body (**John 19:39**).

Just a note:

Essential oils work as a barrier between your skin and germs. For example, when your hand touches a knob after a person with a severe cold has used it. The bacteria seeps directly into your skin. Then the bacteria attaches itself to your skin cells causing you to eventually get sick. When we place essential oils on our hands or skin's surface it creates a barrier and even fights off the bacteria.

The Bible tells us to in **Psalm 39:4** and 1 Peter tells us to count our days. This means get our priorities in order. Monitor how we spend our time. Growing old is a good thing. It's something to look forward too. **Psalm 71:18** informs us that God won't forget us, He has taught us, and if we lived for him we will live longer (**Psalm 94:12**) and obtain gray hair. Gray hair is good. Who knew! If you have gray hair perhaps you are on track with God. I've written the follow information from God's word in a list, because when I'm teaching or making a power point lists help me. I'm sure this will help you too.

1. **Proverbs 16:31**
   Gray hair is a crown of splendor; it is attained in the way of righteousness.

2. **Proverbs 20:29.** The glory of young men is their strength: and the beauty of old men is the gray head.

3. **Proverbs 31:30**
   Give her of the fruit of her hands; and let her own works praise her in the gates

4. **1 Peter 1:24** For, All people are like grass, and all their glory is like the flowers of the field; the grass withers and the flowers fall, but the word of the Lord endures forever And this is the word that was preached to you.

5. **Ecclesiastes 9:7-10** Go, eat your food with gladness, and drink your wine with a joyful heart, for God has already approved what you

do.8 Always be clothed in white, and always anoint your head with oil.9 Enjoy life with your wife, whom you love, all the days of this meaningless life that God has given you under the sun—all your meaningless days. For this is your lot in life and in your toilsome labor under the sun.10 Whatever your hand finds to do, do it with all your might, for in the realm of the dead, where you are going, there is neither working nor planning nor knowledge nor wisdom.

6. **Ecclesiastes 11:9** You who are young, be happy while you are young, and let your heart give you joy in the days of your youth. Follow, the ways of you hear and whatever your eyes see but know that for all these things God will bring you into judgment.

    Ecclesiastes 12:7 (NIV) and the dust returns to the ground it came from, and the spirit returns to God who gave it.

7. 1 **Corinthians 4:16 16** 2 Therefore we do not lose heart. Though, outwardly we are wasting away, yet inwardly we are being renewed day by day.

Growing old is a gift of God! If you consider yourself aging, then be encouraged. God, does not expect you to run around the block for the rest of your life. We are all soldiers on the right team and some of us run, but others may only shout! God expects you to feed the flock. As for me memory is an issue. Don't let little things keep you out of service. No one including Christians, preachers, and singers ever retire! All of us look forward to heaven, but if God has you reading these words He is not done with you! Lean on him more for understanding. If medication is an issue by all means stay with your doctor's plans, but attempt to learn about God's medicine. You be the example!

Study opportunity: Issues that matter and essential oils needed as we age. (In book one, see pages 116-146.This is called class three "Health Issues" (I.E. page 22)

What essential oils help tolerate hot flashes?

Essential oils, blended with peppermint and lemon, will help relieve hot flashes. Since essential oils go right through the skin, applying them to fatty areas of the body where hormones are manufactured and stored will create the most direct effect. Of course, any massage is itself very therapeutic. A bath is also a wonderful way to receive the benefits of these oils.

What Essential Oils help menopause?

These essential oils include clary sage, anise, fennel, cypress, angelica, coriander, sage, and to a lesser degree, basil.

Application: Since essential oils go right through the skin, applying them to fatty areas of the body where hormones are manufactured and stored will create the most direct effect. Fatty areas are sweat glands, scalp, soles of your feet, upper back, ankles, behind the ears, and temples.

What Essential Oils Could Help my Hair Loss?

You can mix essential oils in your shampoo: clary sage, lavender, and melaleuca (Tea Tree) together for great results. They are also suitable for various organic hair masks and they may have different effect on hair condition depending on which natural ingredients you will use.

Are Your Hormones out of control?

If you want to have more balanced hormones, personally, I recommend considering clary sage oil along with thyme oil. For men I recommend the same essential oils, but also add five drops of sandalwood oil. You can just put a few drops on your hand and rub it on your skin.

What Oils Could Improve the function of my heart?

Use basil, rosemary, thyme, marjoram and clove to improve general circulation. Along with marjoram and ginger, these oils also help normalize high blood pressure. As always, remember if you have sensitive skin be sure to mix it with coconut oil. Clove is an essential oil, when applied, produces a burning sensation for some people.

Is your Thyroid a root of evil?

Aromatically, diffusing precise essential (one drop of each in 8oz of distilled water) oils in a diffuser can help energize the body. Frankincense oil also combats the fatigue and sluggishness that often times arrive with low thyroid function. Common, energizing essential oils are cinnamon, eucalyptus, lemon, lime, grapefruit, rosemary and peppermint.

What about PMS symptoms?

During a woman's menstrual cycle, she feels the effects of hormonal imbalances. A number of essential oils can be used to treat the imbalances that accompany 0premenstrual syndrome. For example, aniseed, clary sage, fennel, and sage. All of these have estrogen-like compounds that may make them effective in relieving symptoms associated with PMS.

8. Can you help me find oils to prevent hair loss?
   Essential oils have been ingredients in hair care recipes for generations. Those oils historically have been, Lavender, Chamomile, Rosemary and Melaleuca (Tea Tree). The products have been placed in shampoos and conditioners, because these oils can positively support the health of the hair follicles and scalp. These oils have been said to help the skin on your scalp open pores to absorb and provide a healthy scalp. Most shampoos and conditioners do not have all natural essential oils and if they do they contain only small amounts. So, this is why it would be wise to add them to your personal care items, including your shampoo.

9. What essential oils will help my toothache?
   Try this mouth rinse: chamomile, myrrh, tea tree and peppermint. Simply add 2 drops warm water and wish around your mouth.

If you are teaching this class, you might find this list handy. I use it to assign scriptures. At my church, I wrote the scriptures on the back of some adult Christmas coloring bookmarks.

John 19:40	**2 Corinthians 4:16**
Genesis 24:32	**Psalm 39:4**

Exodus 30:22-25	Psalm 71:18
1 John 4:1	Proverbs 20:29 & 16:31
Ecclesiastes 11:9 & 9:7-10	Ecclesiastes 12:7
1 Peter 1:24	

The following chart includes some more common complaints and its Biblical Antidote.

Complaints	Essential Oils
Stress	Combine the oils with coconut oil and place on the back of the neck. Lavender, lemon, bergamot, peppermint, vetiver, pine, and ylang ylang
Insomnia	Combine the following oils Lavender, Chamomile, jasmine, benzoin, sandalwood oil and ylang ylang; with coconut or avocado oil. Place on bottoms of feet and on your forehead. Defuse or burn the oils in a defuser or candle.
Anxiety	Lavender, bergamot, rose, clary sage, lemon, Roman, chamomile, orange, sandalwood, geranium, and pine All of these oils are good! I create oil wax candles and goat milk soap.
Depressed Mood/Sorrow	Grapefruit, wild orange, tangerine, lemon, and peppermint Mix these oils in your shampoo and anoint yourself while washing your hair.
Pain	Deep Blue, Peppermint, chamomile, lavender, and jasmine

Nausea and vomiting	Mint, ginger, lemon, orange, ginger, dill, fennel, chamomile, clary sage, and lavender Mix with coconut oil and apply to the tummy and belly button.
Tinnitus (Ringing in the Ear)	Aromatherapy experts say that essential oils such as cypress, lemon, rosemary, rose, chamomile and lavender, help to soothe the symptoms and anxieties created by tinnitus. The methods of utilizing essential oils for natural tinnitus relief include vaporization, massage, inhalation, compress and bathing.
High Blood Pressure	Mix several oils, such as rose, lemon, cinnamon, and cassia. Add them to a diffuser or candle. Oil vapor is diffused throughout the air and the scent is inhaled. This olfactory signal is received in the medulla where your blood pressure is controlled in the brain. The smooth muscles that make up the blood vessels relax; thus, lowering blood pressure.
Toenail Fungus	Tea Tree Oil, orange, and lavender. All are both antiseptic and fungicidal remedy. First clean areas on and around the infection with rubbing alcohol then apply undiluted tea tree oil directly to the affected nails and let it soak in.
Neuropathy	Eucalyptus, rosemary, and eucalyptus essential oils are also very helpful in improving diabetic neuropathy symptoms when combined with aloe Vera gel.

CLASS 23

WHO GIVES US THE AUTHORITY TO ANOINT?

SMALL CLASS REVIEW

Please see YouTube for a video of this lesson.

The Bible speaks through the following Scriptures.

Part One: Why essential oils?

_____

_____

_____

    Basically, essential oils were created by God. He said that the vegetation of the world was our food and our medicine.

    In genesis, God gave us trees that created fruit. He said the fruit was for our substance. **Genesis 1:29**

Ezekiel 47:12 said the leaves were for our medicine

Proverbs 107:20 his word heals. Delivered from destruction.

Your Reaction:

_____

_____

_____

Exodus 23:25

25Worship the LORD your God, and his blessing will be on your food and water. I will take away sickness from among you,

Exodus 15:26

26He said, "If you listen carefully to the LORD your God and do what is right in his eyes, if you pay attention to his commands and keep all his decrees, I will not bring on you any of the diseases I brought on the Egyptians, for I am the LORD, who heals you."

> Government can take away our insurance
> But God sent his word to bring our healing and save us from destruction.
> The Bible is life
> It is our health.
> Alternative med is not alterative
> It's God's Medicine

Doctors, scientist agree that we need the power in our food.-But some of them know that the food source was not always available. So, some may have been trying to preserve life, but mostly they wanted to line their pockets with wealth. So, they invented medicine. They took what was free and created a pharmacy. Then they saw that the man-made medicine reacted poorly. Therefore, creating a greater need for more medicine. Thus, creating more wealth for them.

> Gives us authority to heal!
> In **Acts 4:30** He said place hands on them and heal them.
> Disciplines used anointing with oil

James 5:14

14Is anyone among you sick? Let them call the elders of the church to pray over them and anoint them with oil in the name of the LORD.

What results have you witnessed after preforming **James 5:14?**

_____

_____

_____

Mark 6:13

And they cast out many devils, and anointed with oil many that were sick, and healed them.

According to Mark chapter 5, this scripture notifies us that Jesus cast out the demons Legion had inside of himself. Jesus lives in us therefore for can also cast out demons. Where the blood of Jesus is there can be no evil. The word legion is a roman word! The Roman Army used this word to describe the number of members in their ranks. A Roman Leader would often report that we have a legion. Two thousand members would have been the number of men. Therefore, this man had 2,000 or more demons.

The flock of swine (2,000 or more) were not on the hill by accident. They were placed there by God for Jesus to use. Jesus understood the laws of the Jews in their entirety. He understood how pigs were viewed and why. He chose to use the swine, because they were considered the most repulsive animal of their time.

Legion in the man's body asked Jesus permission to enter the swine. See, demons cannot express themselves without a body. Jesus granted the demons permission to indwell the swine, but Jesus chose them to 'drive-home'. Jesus know that the swine would not hold the spirts of the 2,000 demons! The swine could not control themselves. So, they ran downhill! This is an image of sin to me, because when we get involved in sin we often travel a downhill slope. Sin takes us further then we were willing to go. Finally, the drowning of the swine provided a visual explanation of what God wants to do with sin and evil. If you would like more information on this occurrence please obtain a copy of my book entitled, Messages from the Flocks & Herds in God's Backyard.

Acts 11:30

Which also they did, and sent it to the elders by the hands of Barnabas and Saul.

Acts 28:8

And it came to pass, that the father of Publius lay sick of a fever and of a bloody flux: to whom Paul entered in, and prayed, and laid his hands on him, and healed him.

James 5:15

And the prayer of faith shall save the sick, and the Lord shall raise him up; and if he have committed sins, they shall be forgiven him.

Ezekiel 16:6 6"'Then I passed by and saw you kicking about in your blood, and as you lay there in your blood I said to you, "Live!"

This scripture is confusing outside of its context. However, Ezekiel reports how God healed an infant and claims He will do the same for us. Reports of this scripture are all over YouTube. Basically, after a believer affirms this scripture to God and truly believes, God heals. For inspiring video check out YouTube! Finally, my take on the scripture is that this is some persons contact verse. Just like the anointed prayer cloth is ours, because that's what this particular study is considering. Remember, God uses things to create miracles. Thus, this is what my books are all about: Claiming God's words, doing what it says, and believing it in my heart. Friends, that is how healings take place.

Scriptures of Promising Proof!
Believe, Proclaim, and Receive

(Psalms 30:2 NKJV) O LORD my God, I cried out to You, And You healed me.

(Exodus 15:26 NKJV) and said, "If you diligently heed the voice of the LORD your God and do what is right in His sight, give ear to His commandments and keep all His statutes, I will put none of the diseases on you which I have brought on the Egyptians. For I am the LORD who heals you."

Psalms 103:1-4 NKJV Bless the LORD, O my soul; And all that is within me, bless His holy name! {2} Bless the LORD, O my soul, And forget not all His benefits: {3} Who forgives all your iniquities, Who heals all your diseases, {4} Who redeems your life from destruction, Who crowns you with lovingkindness and tender mercies,

Psalms 107:20 NKJV He sent His word and healed them, And delivered them from their destructions.

Psalms 147:3 NKJV He heals the brokenhearted And binds up their wounds.

Proverbs 4:20-22 My son, attend to my words; incline thine ear unto my sayings.21Let them not depart from thine eyes; keep them in the midst of thine heart.22For they are life unto those that find them, and health to all their flesh.

Jeremiah 33:6 Behold, I will bring it health and cure, and I will cure them, and will reveal unto them the abundance of peace and truth.

Matthew 4:23 And Jesus went about all Galilee, teaching in their synagogues, and preaching the gospel of the kingdom, and healing all manner of sickness and all manner of disease among the people. 24And his fame went throughout all Syria: and they brought unto him all sick people that were taken with divers diseases and torments, and those which were possessed with devils, and those which were lunatick, and those that had the palsy; and he healed them.25And there followed him great multitudes of people from Galilee, and from Decapolis, and from Jerusalem, and from Judaea, and from beyond Jordan.

Matthew 10:8 Heal the sick, cleanse the lepers, raise the dead, cast out devils: freely ye have received, freely give.

Examples of what anointing offers Christian Believers!

1. **2 Chronicles**: Soldiers anointed themselves before battle.
   - For Super Natural Power

2. **Luke 22:48**: And Jesus was going into spiritual battle
   Did this to invoke the spirit. -For Super Natural Power

3. **Mark 16:17**, "And these signs shall follow them that believe; In my name shall they cast out devils; they shall speak with new tongues." -Evil must flee

4. **James 2:19** You believe that there is one God; you do well: the devils also believe, and tremble. -Evil can't stay

5. **Hebrews 13:20** Now the God of peace, that brought again from the dead our Lord Jesus, that great shepherd of the sheep, through the blood of the everlasting covenant,
   -Speaks Favor

6. **James 5:14**
   14Is anyone among you sick? Let them call the elders of the church to pray over them and anoint them with oil in the name of the LORD.

   -Speaks Healing

7. **James 1:17** 17Every good and perfect gift is from above, coming down from the Father of the heavenly lights, who does not change like shifting shadows.
   -Gives Blessings

8. **Romans 5:9** Much more then, being now justified by his blood, we shall be saved from wrath through him.
   -Speaks Justification

Review of important concepts from books one and two.

What are essential oils?
What are therapeutic grade oils?
What is aromatherapy & Brain-Barrier?
Prayers for spiritual healing?
What is reflexology?

What are therapeutic grade oils?

We can all agree that each person has an inner most part. **Genesis 2:7** Most people would agree that their innermost part is the soul. The soul is a portion of our body no man can reach. **John 14:6** So, just like human beings' plants have inner most parts too. The Bible does not say plants have a soul, but we can agree that plants have an essence. Just as humans need blood to thrive; **Leviticus 17:11** plants have terpenoids. When you obtain the oils from the leaf's center you have extracted what is known as the precious oils. **Proverbs 21:20** The oil becomes therapeutic grade when the plant is grown in the part of Gods' backyard, where He placed it, **Isiah 40:12** because that is the environment that provides the correct climate and resources for the plant to grow best. Finally, scientist over in France have what they call an **ISO** certification (ISO standards). ISO chemists seem to have the most reliable chemical constituent indicators. Those standards determine whether an essential oil is therapeutic grade or not.

The crucial action in generating a therapeutic grade essential oil is to reserve numerous amounts of delicate aromatic compounds within the oil. Countless numbers of these elements are very fragile and are slaughtered by hot temperature and extraordinary pressure. The process of distillation often is the determining factor in the value of the oil. Essential oil distilling is hard work and somewhat a form of art. The owner of the distillery must understand heat and pressure. If the pressure is too elevated, or the temperature is too extreme, it may change the molecular structure and affect the products fragrance; thus, altering the products chemical constituents.

What is aromatherapy?

God the creator is a remarkable scientist who understand the scientific process of everything that exists in world. **(Revelation 22:13)** Aroma-therapists, botanists, holistic doctors, and reflexologist can be described as the professionals who handle essential oils and therapy. This group of scientist utilize the plant's aroma-producing fragments (essential oils) to treat many different illnesses and diseases. Most Christians recognize 2 **Timothy 3:1** that society requires aroma-therapists and other art forms to explain and model techniques that would lead to better health. Currently, herbalism medicine routinely studies God's backyard to determine what plant can be harvested. Botanists harvest the core of flowers, leaves, stalks, gums, resins, rinds, roots etc. Scientists creatively combine these different substances to create God's medicine. According to **Ezekiel 47:12**, by the river upon the bank thereof, on this side and on that side, shall grow all trees for meat, whose leaf shall not fade, neither shall the fruit thereof be consumed: it shall bring forth new fruit according to his months, because their waters they issued out of the sanctuary: and the fruit thereof shall be for meat, <u>and the leaf thereof for medicine</u>. Subsequently, when Christians combine essential oils with prayer miracles transpire. **James 5:14**

Only chemists, holistic doctors, aroma therapist, and skilled perfumers should combine essential oils. No one else should blend their own concoctions. The best way to educate yourself on the implementation of essential oils is to complete this study, attend a class or two offered by a wellness advocates, doctor visits, examining current research, and by watching educational videos. According to the Bible, **Mark 16:13** The disciples, drove out many demons and anointed many sick people with oil and healed them. Aroma-therapists' are experts at using the essential oils as medicine.1 **John 2:1** Aroma therapist and holistic doctors are proficient. These professionals school the general population on how to implement essential oils in our daily life. For example, through education, society can learn how to use essential oils topically, internally, and by diffusion.

According to aroma therapists, when essential oils are diffused their molecules are absorbed in our air passages creating healing properties for the body. Another clever method to utilize essential oils is by pouring them into bath water. According to many scriptures of the Bible, God's Children used the method of pouring oils onto their bodies. This action of pouring on the oils is similar to the way we pour oils in the bathtub, because in the ancient days there was no running water. I can picture Anna (**Luke 2:37**), Jael (**Judges 4**), Abigail (**1 Samuel 25**), and Lois and Eunice (**2 Timothy 1:5**) pouring in oils of rose and hyssop in their bathes. King Herold had several public pools of water and its been discovered by aerologists. His bathing area included dressing rooms, separate courts for male and female, and he even had some built in his living quarters. He modeled his courts after the Romans. However, in most scriptures the pouring on of oil was done for the purpose of anointing. According to **Exodus 29:7**; Take the anointing oil and anoint him by <u>pouring</u> it on his head. Practitioners of aromatherapy believe, that fragrances in the oils stimulate nerves in the nose. The nerves send impulses to the part of the brain that controls memory and emotion. Christians agree, according to the Bile, that people are healed by the work of the Author **and Perfecter of our Faith. Hebrews 12:2.** Whichever way you believe, I'm glad both ideas merge into one and I have witnessed the benefits of consuming essential oils.

The Great Creator made us distinctively. Therefore, God had to produce several different species of plants. Gods' people extracted essential oils and a blessing from the Father healed multiple sicknesses. According to **Jeremiah 27:5** "Before I formed thee in the belly I knew thee; and before thou camest forth out of the womb I sanctified thee, and I ordained thee a prophet unto the nations." Deliverance from a sickness depends on many differentiations. The formation of each individual person is different; therefore, the results are common, but continually varies between people. The variations depended on the type of essential oil consumed and the symptoms of the patient. The result on the body may have be calming or stimulating. I've witnessed one oil blend working for one person, but not as well on the second person. Thus, this can be explained in God's word, because he made us all different for all different reasons. **Romans 12:6** which it says, "We have different gifts, according to the grace given to each of us. If your gift is prophesying, then prophesy in <u>accordance with your faith</u>. In addition, ORecommended Related to Stress

Managementa couple of theories in science indicate that Stress Symptoms Stress affects us all. You may notice symptoms of stress when disciplining your kids, during busy times at work, when managing your finances, or when coping with a challenging relationship. Stress is everywhere. And while a little stress is OK – some stress is actually beneficial – too much stress can wear you down and make you sick, both mentally and physically. The first step to controlling stress is to know the symptoms of stress. But recognizing stress symptoms may be harder than you think...Read the Stress Symptoms article > > the oils react with the body's hormones and enzymes. Scientists educate that hormones and enzymes can change blood pressures, pulses, and moods. In another scientific theory holistic physicians suggests that the fragrance from several oils may stimulate the body to produce pain-fighting substances. It's because of those theories I began using essential oils. I've witnessed their effectiveness. I quickly realized something was missing. God lead me to the scriptures. I awoke every morning connecting his word and fell asleep in utterance with Jesus. I recommend using essential oils not because scientists promote them, but because God ordained their use.

Prayers for Spiritual Healing

The Good Book explains in Matthew chapter 6 the process and necessity of prayer. Jesus directly instructs us to pray in a certain manner. Matthew 6:9-13 consummates a standard in the method we must pray. First, we ought to know who our Father is and where he lives. We must show admiration for him. Secondly, we should tell him that we worship him with a thankful heart. Thirdly, we should confess our sin. Fourthly, we should deliver our petitions. Finally, we should trust him to care for us and thank him for answering our prayer.

When we pray God occasionally will not listen. For example, **John 9:31** says "Now we know that God heareth not sinners: but if any man be a worshipper of God, and doeth his will, him he heareth." This part of scripture is sour to the belly, but According to **2 Corinthians 6:2 (KJV)** (For he saith, I have heard thee in a time accepted, and in the day of salvation have I succoured thee: behold, now is the accepted time; behold, now is the day of salvation.) The present is the day to be saved. God is everywhere, so we do not have to be at an altar to be saved. God saves people on vacation, at home, in cars, outside, in the hospital, and everywhere. **Romans 10:9** If you declare with your mouth, "Jesus is Lord," and believe in your heart that God raised him from the dead, you will be saved. Then, according to **Isiah 65:24** And it shall come to pass, that before they call, I will answer; and while they are yet speaking, I will hear. This is the best prayer, because God cleans you inside and out. Chirist provides healing for the body, soul, and mind. (**2 Corinthians 5:17**)

In the word, we find an example in Matthew. It's here we find a story of the faith with the Canaanite Woman. **Matthew 15:26-28,** 26 "But Jesus replied, "It is not right to take the children's bread and toss it to the dogs." 27"Yes, Lord, she said, "- even the dogs eat the crumbs that fall from their master's table." 28"O woman," Jesus answered, "your faith is great! Let it be done for you as you desire." And her daughter was healed from that very hour...." The mother requesting Jesus heal her daughter had to "get-right" (repent) before Jesus could heal her daughter. My mother, Becky claims this verse, because all those nights in the hospital, not knowing if I'm coming back from my strokes or not, she spoke to God. – But this verse entered her mind. Thank God he saved her and healed me. I'm sure the women in the verse also felt the same way. If my mother and I only recognized God's medicine at that time. I now understand, I would have received quicker relief of my symptoms, and my mother may not have felt so helpless, because she would have been the applying them to my skin (anointing) and praying

What is Reflexology?

This process of massage is known as a part of science called it scientific reflexology. The hand and foot messages benefit both the olfactory/limbic pathway. Scientific journals note that a touch from another person could boost the mood of another person. Thus, creating emotional benefits from a caring touch.

One of my favorite ways to apply **essential oils** is to simply mix some coconut oil with the essential oil itself and rub it on different areas of the body, according to where it works best for that particular oil. Because essentials oils are so small molecularly, they can actually be absorbed into your body through your skin. So, you can get full body makeover by simply putting essential oils directly on the skin. Below, is a diagram of reflexology.

REFERENCES/RESOURCES

1. *"essential oil". Oxford English Dictionary (online, American English ed.). Retrieved 2014-07-21.*

2. *Reeds, P. J. (2000). "Dispensable and indispensable amino acids for humans". The Journal of Nutrition. 130 (7): 1835S–40S. PMID 10867060.*

3. *Houtsma, M.Th. (1993). E. J. Brill's First Encyclopaedia of Islam, 1913–1936. 4. Brill. pp. 1011–. ISBN 978-90-04-09790-2.*

4. *Gilman, A. G.; Rall, T. W.; Nies, Alan S.; Taylor, Palmer, eds. (1990). Goodman & Gilman's The Pharmacological Basis of Therapeutics (8th ed.). New York: Pergamon. ISBN 0-08-040296-8.* [page needed]

5. *Klaassen, Curtis D.; Amdur, Mary O.; Casarett, Louis J.; Doull, John (1991). Casarett and Doull's Toxicology: The Basic Science of Poisons. New York: McGraw-Hill. ISBN 0071052399.* [page needed]

6. *Ryman, Daniele (1984). The Aromatherapy Handbook: The Secret Healing Power Of Essential Oils. Century Publishing CO. Ltd. pp. Chapter 3. ISBN 9780852072158.*

7. *Aizpurua-Olaizola, Oier; Ormazabal, Markel; Vallejo, Asier; Olivares, Maitane; Navarro, Patricia; Etxebarria, Nestor; Usobiaga, Aresatz (2015-01-01). "Optimization of supercritical fluid consecutive extractions of fatty acids and polyphenols from Vitis vinifera grape wastes". Journal of Food Science. 80 (1): E101–107. doi:10.1111/1750-3841.12715. ISSN 1750-3841. PMID 25471637.*

8. *Forster, P; et al. (2007). "Changes in Atmospheric Constituents and in Radiative Forcing" (PDF). In Solomon, S; et al. Climate Change 2007: The Physical Science Basis. Contribution of Working Group I to the Fourth Assessment Report of the Intergovernmental Panel on Climate Change. Cambridge University Press.*

9. *Refrigerant 1234YF's Potential Impact in Automotive Applications* [full citation needed]

10. *"ISO TC 54 Business Plan – Essential oils" (PDF). Retrieved 2006-09-14.* It is unclear from the source what period of time the quoted figures include.

11. *"Carvacrol data sheet from Sigma-Aldrich".*

12. Soares, I.H.; Loreto, É.S.; Rossato, L.; Mario, D.N.; Venturini, T.P.; Baldissera, F.; Santurio, J.M.; Alves, S.H. (2015). "In vitro activity of essential oils extracted from condiments against fluconazole-resistant and -sensitive Candida glabrata". Journal de Mycologie Médicale / Journal of Medical Mycology. 25 (3): 213–7. doi:10.1016/j.mycmed.2015.06.003. PMID 26281965.

13. Mandras, Narcisa; Nostro, Antonia; Roana, Janira; Scalas, Daniela; Banche, Giuliana; Ghisetti, Valeria; Del Re, Simonetta; Fucale, Giacomo; Cuffini, Anna Maria; Tullio, Vivian (2016). "Liquid and vapour-phase antifungal activities of essential oils against Candida albicans and non-albicans Candida". BMC Complementary and Alternative Medicine. 16 (1): 330. doi:10.1186/s12906-016-1316-5. PMC 5006570 . PMID 27576581.

14. ^ Jump up to: a b Sapeika, Norman (1963). Actions and Uses of Drugs. A.A. Balkema. |page needed|

15. Haneke, Karen E (February 2002), Turpentine (Turpentine Oil, Wood Turpentine, Sulfate Turpentine, Sulfite Turpentine) [8006-64-2]: Review of Toxicological Literature (PDF) (Contract No. N01–ES–65402), National Institute of Environmental Health Sciences |page needed|

16. Watt, John Mitchell; Breyer-Brandwijk, Maria Gerdina (1962). The Medicinal and Poisonous Plants of Southern and Eastern Africa (2nd ed.). Edinburgh: E & S Livingstone. |page needed|

17. Levy, Stuart B. (2001). "Antibacterial Household Products: Cause for Concern". Emerging Infectious Diseases. 7 (7): 512–5. doi:10.3201/eid0707.017705. PMC 2631814 PMID 11485643.

18. Singh, G.; Kapoor, I. P. S.; Pandey, S. K.; Singh, U. K.; Singh, R. K. (2002). "Studies on essential oils: Part 10; Antibacterial activity of volatile oils of some spices". Phytotherapy Research. 16 (7): 680–2. doi:10.1002/ptr.951. PMID 12410554.

19. Larson, David; Jacob, Sharon E. (2012). "Tea Tree Oil". Dermatitis. 23 (1): 48–9. doi:10.1097/DER.0b013e31823e202d. PMID 22653070.

20. ^ Jump up to: a b Trattner, Akiva; David, Michael; Lazarov, Aneta (2008). "Occupational contact dermatitis due to essential oils". Contact Dermatitis. 58 (5): 282–4. doi:10.1111/j.1600-0536.2007.01275.x. PMID 18416758.

21. ^ Jump up to: *a b* Bleasel, Narelle; Tate, Bruce; Rademaker, Marius (2002). *"Allergic contact dermatitis following exposure to essential oils"*. Australasian Journal of Dermatology. **43** *(3): 211–3. doi:10.1046/j.1440-0960.2002.00598.x. PMID 12121401.*

22. ^ Jump up to: *a b* Isaksson, M; Brandão, F. M.; Bruze, M; Goossens, A (2000). *"Short Communications"*. Contact Dermatitis. **43** *(1): 41–2. doi:10.1034/j.1600-0536.2000.043001041.x. PMID 10902588.*

23. Lee, Myeong Soo; Choi, Jiae; Posadzki, Paul; Ernst, Edzard (2012). *"Aromatherapy for health care: An overview of systematic reviews"*. Maturitas. **71** *(3): 257–60. doi:10.1016/j.maturitas.2011.12.018. PMID 22285469.*

24. Posadzki, P; Alotaibi, A; Ernst, E (2012). *"Adverse effects of aromatherapy: A systematic review of case reports and case series"*. The International journal of risk & safety in medicine. **24** *(3): 147–61. doi:10.3233/JRS-2012-0568 (inactive 2017-04-02). PMID 22936057.*

25. https://charcoaloil.com/collections/carrier-oils

26. Copyright 2009 - 2017 www.your-aromatherapy-guide.com

27. Axelsson, J., Sundelin, T., Ingre, M., Van Someren, E. J., Olsson, A., & Lekander, M. (2010). Beauty sleep: Experimental study on the perceived health and attractiveness of sleep deprived people. *British Medical Journal, 341,* 1287-1289.

28. Buss, D. M. (1988). The evolution of human intrasexual competition: tactics of mate attraction. *Journal of Personality and Social Psychology, 54,* 616-628.

29. Buss, D. M., & Barnes, M. (1986).Preferences in human mate selection. *Journal of Personality and Social Psychology, 50,* 559-570.

30. Dion, K., Berscheid, E., & Walster, E. (1972). What is beautiful is good. *Journal of Personality and Social Psychology, 24,* 285-290

31. Gordon, A. M. & Chen, S. (2014). The role of sleep in interpersonal conflict: Do sleepless nights mean worse fights? *Social Psychological and Personality Science, 5,* 168-175. quality and the marital bed: Examining the covariation between relationship quality and sleep. *Sleep Medicine Reviews, 11,* 389-404.

32. De Vaux, Anc Isr, 56–61 (incl bibl. p. 523); Callaway, in: BA, 26 (1963), 74–91; Bender, in: JQR, 6 (1894), 317–47, 664–71; 7 (1895), 101–18, 259–69; J.J.

33. Greenwald (Grunwald), *Kol Bo al Avelut* (1947); H. Rabinowicz, *Guide to Life* (1964)

34. J.M. Tykocinski, *Gesher ha-Hayyim* (1944); S. Freehof, *Current Reform Response* (1969), index.

35. References:

36. Z. Wlodarczyk, "Review of Plant Species Cited in the Bible," Folia Horticulturae, vol. 19, no. 1, pp. 67-85, 2007.

37. M. C. Tenney, The Zondervan Pictorial Bible Dictionary, Michigan: Zondervan Publishing House, 1974.

38. R. C. Brettell, E. M. Schotsmans, P. Walton Rogers, N. Reifarth, R. C. Redfern, B. Stern and C. P. Heron, "'Choicest unguents': Molecular Evidence for the Use of Resinous Plant Exudates in Late Roman Mortuary Rites in Britain," Journal of Archaeological Science, vol. 53, pp. 639-648, 2015.

39. C. Aling, "Joseph in Egypt: Part 1," Associates for Biblical Research, 18 February 2010. [Online]. Available: http://www.biblearchaeology. org/post/2010/02/18/Joseph-in-Egypt-Part-I.aspx#Article. [Accessed 14 June 2017].

40. G. Abdel-Maksoud and A.-R. El-Amin, "A Review on the Materials used During the Mummification Processes in Anicent Egypt," Mediterranean Archeaology and Archaeometry, vol. 11, no. 2, pp. 129-150, 2011.

41. G. W. Van Beek, "Frankincense and Myrrh," The Biblical Archaeologist, vol. 23, no. 3, pp. 69-95, 1960

Printed in the United States
By Bookmasters